The Ultimate
Air Fryer Cookbook
2023 UK

1200 Days Quick, Healthy and Budget-Friendly Air Fryer

Recipes For Smart People to Improve Everyday Diet at Ease

Wilburn Heidenreich

Table of Contents

Introduction 1

Chapter 1 Dive Into the Air Fryer 2
What Makes the Air Fryer So Special? 3
What Kinds of Air Fryers Are There For Me to Choose From? 4
Air Fryer Tips and Tricks! 5
Air Fryer FAQs 5

Chapter 2 Breakfasts 6
Taco-Spiced Chickpeas 7
Poutine with Waffle Fries 7
Shrimp Toasts with Sesame Seeds 7
Kale Chips with Sesame 7
Dark Chocolate and Cranberry Granola Bars 7
Lemony Endive in Curried Yoghurt 8
Mushroom Tarts 8
Jalapeño Poppers 8
Shishito Peppers with Herb Dressing 8
Spicy Chicken Bites 8
Red Pepper Tapenade 9
Goat Cheese and Garlic Crostini 9
Feta and Quinoa Stuffed Mushrooms 9
Greek Yoghurt Devilled Eggs 9
Tortellini with Spicy Dipping Sauce 9
Sea Salt Potato Crisps 9
Polenta Fries with Chilli-Lime Mayo 10
Golden Onion Rings 10
Cheese-Stuffed Blooming Onion 10
Fried Artichoke Hearts 10
Onion Pakoras 11
Veggie Shrimp Toast 11
Shrimp Pirogues 11
Lemon-Pepper Chicken Drumsticks 11
Sweet Potato Fries with Mayonnaise 11
Kale Chips with Tex-Mex Dip 12
Beef and Mango Skewers 12
Ranch Oyster Snack Crackers 12
Root Veggie Chips with Herb Salt 12
Rosemary-Garlic Shoestring Fries 12

Chapter 3 Breakfasts 13
Savory Sweet Potato Hash 14
Broccoli-Mushroom Frittata 14
White Bean–Oat Waffles 14
Turkey Breakfast Sausage Patties 14
Breakfast Meatballs 14
Cheddar Soufflés 15
Gluten-Free Granola Cereal 15
Mississippi Spice Muffins 15
Apple Rolls 15
Egg Tarts 15
Portobello Eggs Benedict 16
Jalapeño Popper Egg Cups 16
Spinach and Mushroom Mini Quiche 16
Mushroom-and-Tomato Stuffed Hash Browns 16
Homemade Cherry Breakfast Tarts 16
Mexican Breakfast Pepper Rings 17
Homemade Toaster Pastries 17
Southwestern Ham Egg Cups 17
Golden Avocado Tempura 17
Cinnamon-Raisin Bagels 17
Buffalo Chicken Breakfast Muffins 17
Egg and Bacon Muffins 18
Scotch Eggs 18
Wholemeal Banana-Walnut Bread 18
Cheddar-Ham-Corn Muffins 18
Ham and Cheese Crescents 18
Classic British Breakfast 18
Maple Granola 19
Double-Dipped Mini Cinnamon Biscuits 19
Bacon, Egg, and Cheese Roll Ups 19
Honey-Apricot Granola with Greek Yoghurt 19
Oat Bran Muffins 20
Cauliflower Avocado Toast 20
Fried Chicken Wings with Waffles 20
Banana-Nut Muffins 20

Chapter 4 Pizzas, Wraps, and Sandwiches 21
Crispy Chicken Egg Rolls 22
Spinach and Ricotta Pockets 22
Portobello Pizzas 22
Cheesy Veggie Wraps 22
English Muffin Tuna Sandwiches 23
Korean Flavour Beef and Onion Tacos 23
Barbecue Chicken Pitta Pizza 23
Bacon and Pepper Sandwiches 23
Mexican Flavour Chicken Burgers 23
Jerk Chicken Wraps 24
Grilled Cheese Sandwich 24
Bacon Garlic Pizza 24
Beans and Greens Pizza 24
Mediterranean-Pitta Wraps 24
Nugget and Veggie Taco Wraps 24
Air Fried Philly Cheesesteaks 25
Barbecue Pulled Pork Sandwiches 25
Pesto Chicken Mini Pizzas 25
Tuna Wraps 25
Beef and Pepper Fajitas 25

Chapter 5 Vegetables and Sides 26

Baked Jalapeño and Cheese Cauliflower Mash 27
Spinach and Sweet Pepper Poppers 27
Curried Fruit 27
Courgette Balls 27
Blistered Shishito Peppers with Lime Juice 27
Tingly Chili-Roasted Broccoli 27
Roasted Radishes with Sea Salt 28
Cauliflower with Lime Juice 28
Garlic Courgette and Red Peppers 28
Dill-and-Garlic Beetroots 28
Garlic Cauliflower with Tahini 28
Sweet and Crispy Roasted Pearl Onions 28
Bacon Potatoes and Green Beans 28
Gold Artichoke Hearts 29
Asparagus Fries 29

Flatbread 29
Dijon Roast Cabbage 29
Creamed Asparagus 29
Roasted Brussels Sprouts with Bacon 29
Broccoli-Cheddar Twice-Baked Potatoes 30
Air Fried Potatoes with Olives 30
"Faux-Tato" Hash 30
Crispy Garlic Sliced Aubergine 30
Five-Spice Roasted Sweet Potatoes 30
Curry Roasted Cauliflower 30
Mole-Braised Cauliflower 31
Asian Tofu Salad 31
Corn and Coriander Salad 31
Brussels Sprouts with Pecans and Gorgonzola 31
Sweet-and-Sour Brussels Sprouts 32

Chapter 6 Poultry 33

Chicken and Vegetable Fajitas 34
Thai Tacos with Peanut Sauce 34
Breaded Turkey Cutlets 34
Spice-Rubbed Chicken Thighs 34
South Indian Pepper Chicken 35
Piri-Piri Chicken Thighs 35
Crispy Dill Chicken Strips 35
Chicken Rochambeau 35
Chicken Nuggets 36
One-Dish Chicken and Rice 36
Nashville Hot Chicken 36
Coconut Chicken Meatballs 36
Chicken Patties 36
Bacon-Wrapped Chicken Breasts Rolls 37
Chicken Breasts with Asparagus, Beans, and Rocket ... 37
Korean Honey Wings 37
Barbecued Chicken with Creamy Coleslaw 37
Chicken and Gruyère Cordon Bleu 38
Thai Chicken with Cucumber and Chili Salad 38
Thai-Style Cornish Game Hens 38

Chicken with Lettuce 38
Pomegranate-Glazed Chicken with Couscous Salad 39
Buttermilk-Fried Drumsticks 39
Peanut Butter Chicken Satay 39
Gochujang Chicken Wings 39
Chicken Croquettes with Creole Sauce 40
Coconut Chicken Wings with Mango Sauce 40
Crunchy Chicken Tenders 40
Tex-Mex Chicken Roll-Ups 40
Thai Curry Meatballs 41
Spanish Chicken and Mini Sweet Pepper Baguette 41
African Merguez Meatballs 41
Lemon Thyme Roasted Chicken 41
Turkey Meatloaf 41
Easy Cajun Chicken Drumsticks 42
Chicken Drumsticks with Barbecue-Honey Sauce 42
Pork Rind Fried Chicken 42
Air Fried Chicken Potatoes with Sun-Dried Tomato 42
Smoky Chicken Leg Quarters 42
Chicken Schnitzel 43

Chapter 7 Beef, Pork, and Lamb 44

Currywurst 45
Pork Schnitzels with Sour Cream and Dill Sauce 45
Goat Cheese-Stuffed Bavette Steak 45
Beefy Poppers 45
Ritzy Skirt Steak Fajitas 46
Garlic Butter Steak Bites 46
Tuscan Air Fried Veal Loin 46
Mexican-Style Shredded Beef 46
Cheddar Bacon Burst with Spinach 46
Pork Loin with Aloha Salsa 47
Almond and Caraway Crust Steak 47
Five-Spice Pork Belly 47
Sausage and Peppers 47
Filipino Crispy Pork Belly 47
Sirloin Steak with Honey-Mustard Butter 48

Pork Bulgogi 48
Spicy Rump Steak 48
Bone-in Pork Chops 48
Pork and Beef Egg Rolls 48
Rack of Lamb with Pistachio Crust 49
Savory Sausage Cobbler 49
Fillet with Crispy Shallots 49
Panko Pork Chops 49
Sausage and Cauliflower Arancini 50
Cheesy Low-Carb Lasagna 50
Spice-Rubbed Pork Loin 50
Parmesan Herb Filet Mignon 50
Mexican Pork Chops 50
Lamb Chops with Horseradish Sauce 51
Beef and Tomato Sauce Meatloaf 51

Chapter 8 Fish and Seafood 52

Catfish Bites 53
Tuna Avocado Bites 53
Roasted Halibut Steaks with Parsley 53
Cayenne Sole Cutlets 53
Seasoned Tuna Steaks 53
Bacon Halibut Steak 53
Orange-Mustard Glazed Salmon 54
Lemon Pepper Prawns 54
South Indian Fried Fish 54
Prawn and Cherry Tomato Kebabs 54
Lemony Prawns and Courgette 54
Sweet Tilapia Fillets 55
chilli Tilapia 55
Asian Marinated Salmon 55
Crispy Fish Sticks 55

Crab Cakes with Bell Peppers 55
Tuna and Fruit Kebabs 55
Salmon on Bed of Fennel and Carrot 56
Air Fryer Fish Fry 56
Garlic Prawns 56
Country Prawns 56
Stuffed Sole Florentine 56
Maple Balsamic Glazed Salmon 57
Honey-Balsamic Salmon 57
Lemony Prawns 57
Cod Tacos with Mango Salsa 57
Bang Bang Prawns 57
Black Cod with Grapes and Kale 58
Lemony Salmon 58
Snapper with Fruit 58

Chapter 9 Holiday Specials 59

Classic Latkes 60
Custard Donut Holes with Chocolate Glaze 60
Simple Butter Cake 60
Golden Salmon and Carrot Croquettes 60
Eggnog Bread 61
Simple Baked Green Beans 61
Jewish Blintzes 61
Hearty Honey Yeast Rolls 61
Teriyaki Shrimp Skewers 61
South Carolina Shrimp and Corn Bake 62

Frico 62
Arancini 62
Fried Dill Pickles with Buttermilk Dressing 62
Spicy Air Fried Old Bay Shrimp 62
Simple Air Fried Crispy Brussels Sprouts 63
Easy Cinnamon Toast 63
Crispy Potato Chips with Lemony Cream Dip 63
Garlicky Baked Cherry Tomatoes 63
Lemony and Garlicky Asparagus 63
Garlicky Zoodles 63

Chapter 10 Desserts 64

Strawberry Shortcake 65
Cinnamon Cupcakes with Cream Cheese Frosting .. 65
Pecan Brownies 65
Strawberry Pastry Rolls 65
Baked Brazilian Pineapple 66
Gluten-Free Spice Cookies 66
Pecan Bars 66
Pecan Butter Cookies 66
Old-Fashioned Fudge Pie 66
Caramelized Fruit Skewers 66
Cream Cheese Danish 67
Shortcut Spiced Apple Butter 67
Lemon Curd Pavlova 67

Almond Shortbread 67
Pecan and Cherry Stuffed Apples 67
Butter Flax Cookies 68
Almond-Roasted Pears 68
Biscuit-Base Cheesecake 68
Apple Wedges with Apricots 68
Molten Chocolate Almond Cakes 68
Chickpea Brownies 69
Berry Crumble 69
Applesauce and Chocolate Brownies 69
Apple Hand Pies 69
Homemade Mint Pie 69

Chapter 11 Staples, Sauces, Dips, and Dressings 70

Traditional Caesar Dressing 71
Cucumber Yoghurt Dip 71
Hot Honey Mustard Dip 71
Tzatziki 71
Dijon and Balsamic Vinaigrette 71
Tomatillo Salsa for Air Fryer 71

Lemon Cashew Dip 72
Air Fryer Artichoke Dip 72
Cauliflower Alfredo Sauce 72
Apple Cider Dressing 72

INTRODUCTION

The air fryer took the cooking appliance market by storm in 2007 when first introduced by Tefal in the form of their Actifry range. It took the concept of the previously familiar convection oven and elevated it to the next level. There were popular elements that were retained, including the convenience of a hands-free approach, whereby we can leave our food largely unattended cooking in the air fryer to focus on the other million things happening in the kitchen. But the improvements made using the air fryer technology put it in a whole new league above the traditional convection oven.

There was the increased speed of cooking- gone were the days of impatiently waiting for the oven to preheat, followed by up to an hour of slowly baking your food. The air fryer is so much more efficient, making it perfect for breakfasts on the go - I remember during the pandemic when everyone brought their own meals to work, I was so thankful to the air fryer for giving me some extra time to sleep before waking up to quickly prepare and pack my food, even while groggy from sleep! If I can use it even before my morning cup of coffee, you definitely would not have any problems with it too!

It was also able to replicate the taste and texture of deep fried foods in a way that the oven was never quite able to achieve. I've definitely tried to make some home-made chips in the oven, only to end up with semi-soggy potatoes with none of the satisfying crunch I was looking for in a chip. On others days, I've tried to re-heat some leftover chicken katsu in the microwave, only to be disappointed by how different it tasted without it's crispy breading. Ever since getting a microwave, neither of these issues have bothered me again.

With it's convenience, efficiency and unique ability to give us healthy yet delicious fried food, it does not come as a surprise to any that the air fryer enjoys unparalleled popularity, and is even considered a kitchen staple in many households, including mine! It has made cooking so much easier more accessible, even for complete beginners in the kitchen.

This cookbook will introduce some easy-to-follow recipes suitable for cooks of every skill level, from experienced home cooks just looking for new ideas and inspiration, to beginners who are testing out their brand-new air fryers!

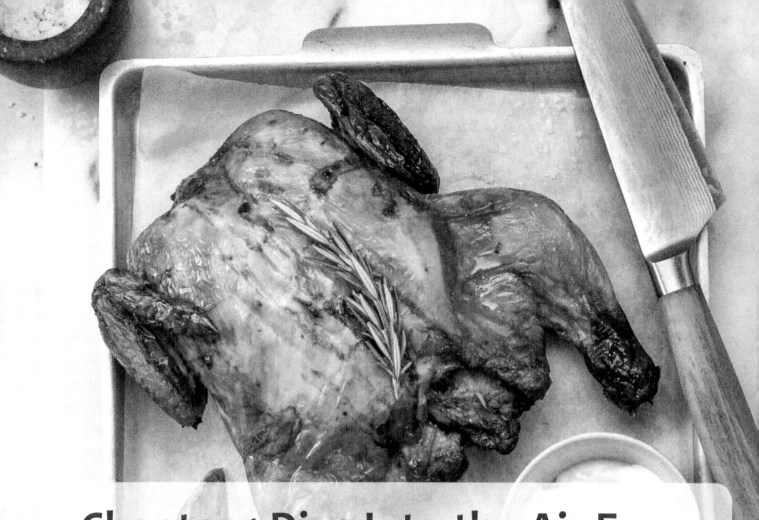

Chapter 1 Dive Into the Air Fryer

Chapter 1 Dive Into the Air Fryer

You can view the air fryer as an upgraded, table-top version of the convection oven. The basis of it's technology is the same - if we can circulate hot air around our food within a confined area and at a quick enough pace, we can cook it. However, the browning reactions, such as the Maillard reaction, which gives us the beautiful crust on pan-fried or deep-fried foods, can only occur at sufficiently high speeds, which aren't always attainable in larger and weaker ovens. The air fryer overcomes these issues, hence replicating deep-fried textures without the hassle and negative health impacts of actually deep frying our foods.

What Makes the Air Fryer So Special?

Less Fat

Deep frying methods submerge our food in hot oil, causing them to absorb a significant amount of the oil, which contains high amounts of saturated fats and trans fats. Both these fats are extremely detrimental to our health, particular when consumed in excess. The air fryer creates fried food with significantly lesser fat content by excluding the large amounts of oil, and instead uses hot air to bring the required heat to our food.

Faster Meals

The hot air in air fryers are circulated at speeds up to 70km/h - can you imagine that? At such high speeds, and at temperatures up to 200°C, it's no wonder that the air fryer can complete some of the same meals as in an oven in less than half the time! The user-friendly controls also reduces any confusion as to what setting to use, or how to set a temperature. Such efficient technology and simple design allows us to whip up whole meals in the span of minutes!

More Meal Choices

Let your creative juices flow when using the air fryer. Be it for sides like chips or roasted vegetables, or mains like meatballs and fried chicken, or even desserts, the possibilities are endless when it comes to the meal choices available with the air fryer. Being a relatively new introduction to people's kitchens, there is rapid innovation in this market, with new recipes and ideas springing up on social media and cookbooks (such as this!) everyday.

Less Energy

It might come as a shock to you to know that air fryers actually consume less energy than traditional ovens, despite it's superior strength and efficiency. Its smaller size means that it heats up faster, and the shorter cook time also means that it doesn't have to remain turned on for as long of a time to complete the same meal. With rising energy prices, the lower energy usage may also result in greater savings for your household!

Enough Capacity

There are air fryers of varying sizes to suit different capacity needs- they can be perfect for single person meals while also being large enough to complete dishes for the whole family. Let's be honest, we've nearly never used more than one rack in the oven any given time. The air fryer, despite its compact counter-top friendly size, can still give us sufficient capacity to serve all our cooking needs.

What Kinds of Air Fryers Are There For Me to Choose From?

There are many different types of air fryers currently available on the market, each with their own distinctive set of features. Here are some more popular ranges that you would probably find, and each of their defining characteristics:

Instant Vortex Plus Dual Air Fryer

This air fryer has two baskets, allowing you to make two completely different dishes at the same time. They also come with a transparent door that allows you to look into the baskets even when they're closed, so you can keep a close eye on the progress of your food.

Cosori Dual Blaze Smart Air Fryer

This option is likely the most high-tech and comes with an accompanying app from which you can find recipes and remotely control the machine, even if you're in a completely different room. It also comes with 13 different modes for all kinds of food.

Lakeland Digital Compact Air Fryer

As you can probably tell from its name, this air fryer is perfect for smaller kitchen tabletops, and can easily be kept away when not in use. Despite its smaller size, it still has a sizable capacity of 1.6L and comes with 5 pre-programmed functions.

Ninja AF160UK Air Fryer Ma 5.2L

For larger households, this high-capacity air fryer is perfect for making meals large enough for the whole family. It also has a highly developed baking function, making it perfect even for baking whole cakes. With a dishwasher safe, non-stick coated basket base, clean up is also made easy.

Tefal ActiFry Genius XL 2-in-1 Air Fryer

This evolution of the original ActiFry includes a new feature that collects and reuses the oil and fat released by foods during the entire cooking process, reducing the amount of oil required while maximising crisp. The multi-layer design also allows multiple food items to be cooked concurrently.

Air Fryer Tips and Tricks!

Don't overcrowd the basket

It is vital that each item in the basket has enough space for the hot air to come into contact with it and crisp it up. This will also ensure even cooking each time.

Don't cover the heating element or fan

Placing aluminum foil or baking paper below your food makes clean up easier, but always make sure that they do not cover the heating element or the fan. Each air fryer might have a different placement of these elements, so check your instruction manual to avoid this mistake!

Weigh down loose pieces

With air moving at such high speeds, it's easy for lighter or unsecured foods to get blown around within the air fryer. Trim off loose pieces or secure them with a toothpick to keep your food in one piece!

Air Fryer FAQs

Q: Do I still need to put any oil on my food?

A: You can spray a small amount of oil on your food with an oil spray bottle to get an extra crunch and taste. Just a small amount would suffice, and you can rely on the air fryer to do the rest.

Q: Can I open the air fryer in the middle of its cooking time?

A: Of course you can! The air fryer should have safety mechanisms in place to stop the process when the basket is opened, and you can safely check on the progress of your food. Once the process is resumed, it'll be as if no disruption had occurred!

Q: Can you bake cookies and other pastries in the air fryer?

A: Yes, but do make sure that the recipe is air fryer compatible. Pastries can come out extra delicious from the air fryer, with a beautiful crust and amazing texture. Wet batter baked goods, like cookies, may need to be tweaked, but can definitely still be done!

Q: Can I use oven recipes in the air fryer?

A: Yes, but make sure to set your air fryer temperature to 15-30°C below the temperature recommended for convectional ovens, and reduce your cook time by half. However, do make sure to still keep an eye on your food and adjust the temperature and time accordingly!

Chapter 2 Snacks and Appetisers

Chapter 2 Snacks and Appetisers

Taco-Spiced Chickpeas

Prep time: 5 minutes | Cook time: 17 minutes | Serves 3

Oil, for spraying
1 (439 g) can chickpeas, drained
1 teaspoon chilli powder
½ teaspoon ground cumin
½ teaspoon salt
½ teaspoon granulated garlic
2 teaspoons lime juice

Line the air fryer basket with parchment and spray lightly with oil. Place the chickpeas in the prepared basket. Air fry at 200°C for 17 minutes, shaking or stirring the chickpeas and spraying lightly with oil every 5 to 7 minutes. In a small bowl, mix together the chilli powder, cumin, salt, and garlic. When 2 to 3 minutes of cooking time remain, sprinkle half of the seasoning mix over the chickpeas. Finish cooking. Transfer the chickpeas to a medium bowl and toss with the remaining seasoning mix and the lime juice. Serve immediately.

Poutine with Waffle Fries

Prep time: 10 minutes | Cook time: 15 to 17 minutes | Serves 4

475 ml frozen waffle cut fries
2 teaspoons olive oil
1 red pepper, chopped
2 spring onions, sliced
240 ml shredded Swiss cheese
120 ml bottled chicken gravy

Preheat the air fryer to 192°C. Toss the waffle fries with the olive oil and place in the air fryer basket. Air fry for 10 to 12 minutes, or until the fries are crisp and light golden brown, shaking the basket halfway through the cooking time. Transfer the fries to a baking pan and top with the pepper, spring onions, and cheese. Air fry for 3 minutes, or until the vegetables are crisp and tender. Remove the pan from the air fryer and drizzle the gravy over the fries. Air fry for 2 minutes, or until the gravy is hot. Serve immediately.

Shrimp Toasts with Sesame Seeds

Prep time: 15 minutes | Cook time: 6 to 8 minutes | Serves 4 to 6

230 g raw shrimp, peeled and deveined
1 egg, beaten
2 spring onions, chopped, plus more for garnish
2 tablespoons chopped fresh coriander
2 teaspoons grated fresh ginger
1 to 2 teaspoons sriracha sauce
1 teaspoon soy sauce
½ teaspoon toasted sesame oil
6 slices thinly sliced white sandwich bread
120 ml sesame seeds
Cooking spray
Thai chilli sauce, for serving

Preheat the air fryer to 204°C. Spritz the air fryer basket with cooking spray. In a food processor, add the shrimp, egg, spring onions, coriander, ginger, sriracha sauce, soy sauce and sesame oil, and pulse until chopped finely. You'll need to stop the food processor occasionally to scrape down the sides. Transfer the shrimp mixture to a bowl. On a clean work surface, cut the crusts off the sandwich bread. Using a brush, generously brush one side of each slice of bread with shrimp mixture. Place the sesame seeds on a plate. Press bread slices, shrimp-side down, into sesame seeds to coat evenly. Cut each slice diagonally into quarters. Spread the coated slices in a single layer in the air fryer basket. Air fry in batches for 6 to 8 minutes, or until golden and crispy. Flip the bread slices halfway through. Repeat with the remaining bread slices. Transfer to a plate and let cool for 5 minutes. Top with the chopped spring onions and serve warm with Thai chilli sauce.

Kale Chips with Sesame

Prep time: 15 minutes | Cook time: 8 minutes | Serves 5

2 L deribbed kale leaves, torn into 2-inch pieces
1½ tablespoons olive oil
¾ teaspoon chilli powder
¼ teaspoon garlic powder
½ teaspoon paprika
2 teaspoons sesame seeds

Preheat air fryer to 176°C. In a large bowl, toss the kale with the olive oil, chilli powder, garlic powder, paprika, and sesame seeds until well coated. Put the kale in the air fryer basket and air fry for 8 minutes, flipping the kale twice during cooking, or until the kale is crispy. Serve warm.

Dark Chocolate and Cranberry Granola Bars

Prep time: 5 minutes | Cook time: 15 minutes | Serves 6

475 ml certified gluten-free quick oats
2 tablespoons sugar-free dark chocolate chunks
2 tablespoons unsweetened dried cranberries
3 tablespoons unsweetened shredded coconut
120 ml raw honey
1 teaspoon ground cinnamon
⅛ teaspoon salt
2 tablespoons olive oil

Preheat the air fryer to 182°C. Line an 8-by-8-inch baking dish with parchment paper that comes up the side so you can lift it out after cooking. In a large bowl, mix together all of the ingredients until well combined. Press the oat mixture into the pan in an even layer. Place the pan into the air fryer basket and bake for 15 minutes. Remove the pan from the air fryer and lift the granola cake out of the pan using the edges of the parchment paper. Allow to cool for 5 minutes before slicing into 6 equal bars. Serve immediately or wrap in plastic wrap and store at room temperature for up to 1 week.

Lemony Endive in Curried Yoghurt

Prep time: 5 minutes | Cook time: 10 minutes | Serves 6

6 heads endive
120 ml plain and fat-free yoghurt
3 tablespoons lemon juice
1 teaspoon garlic powder
½ teaspoon curry powder
Salt and ground black pepper, to taste

Wash the endives and slice them in half lengthwise. In a bowl, mix together the yoghurt, lemon juice, garlic powder, curry powder, salt and pepper. Brush the endive halves with the marinade, coating them completely. Allow to sit for at least 30 minutes or up to 24 hours. Preheat the air fryer to 160ºC. Put the endives in the air fryer basket and air fry for 10 minutes. Serve hot.

Mushroom Tarts

Prep time: 15 minutes | Cook time: 38 minutes | Makes 15 tarts

2 tablespoons extra-virgin olive oil, divided
1 small white onion, sliced
227 g shiitake mushrooms, sliced
¼ teaspoon sea salt
¼ teaspoon freshly ground black pepper
60 ml dry white wine
1 sheet frozen puff pastry, thawed
240 ml shredded Gruyère cheese
Cooking oil spray
1 tablespoon thinly sliced fresh chives

Insert the crisper plate into the basket and the basket into the unit. Preheat the unit by selecting BAKE, setting the temperature to 148ºC, and setting the time to 3 minutes. Select START/STOP to begin. In a heatproof bowl that fits into the basket, stir together 1 tablespoon of olive oil, the onion, and the mushrooms. Once the unit is preheated, place the bowl into the basket. Select BAKE, set the temperature to 148ºC, and set the time to 7 minutes. Select START/STOP to begin. After about 2½ minutes, stir the vegetables. Resume cooking. After another 2½ minutes, the vegetables should be browned and tender. Season with the salt and pepper and add the wine. Resume cooking until the liquid evaporates, about 2 minutes. When the cooking is complete, place the bowl on a heatproof surface. Increase the air fryer temperature to 200ºC and set the time to 3 minutes. Select START/STOP to begin. Unfold the puff pastry and cut it into 15 (3-by-3-inch) squares. Using a fork, pierce the dough and brush both sides with the remaining 1 tablespoon of olive oil. Evenly distribute half the cheese among the puff pastry squares, leaving a ½-inch border around the edges. Divide the mushroom-onion mixture among the pastry squares and top with the remaining cheese. 1Once the unit is preheated, spray the crisper plate with cooking oil. Working in batches, place 5 tarts into the basket; do not stack or overlap. 1Select BAKE, set the temperature to 200ºC, and set the time to 8 minutes. Select START/STOP to begin. 1After 6 minutes, check the tarts; if not yet golden brown, resume cooking for about 2 minutes more. 1When the cooking is complete, remove the tarts and transfer to a wire rack to cool. Repeat steps 10, 11, and 12 with the remaining tarts. 1Serve garnished with the chives.

Jalapeño Poppers

Prep time: 10 minutes | Cook time: 20 minutes | Serves 4

Oil, for spraying
227 g soft white cheese
177 ml gluten-free breadcrumbs, divided
2 tablespoons chopped fresh
parsley
½ teaspoon granulated garlic
½ teaspoon salt
10 jalapeño peppers, halved and seeded

Line the air fryer basket with parchment and spray lightly with oil. In a medium bowl, mix together the soft white cheese, half of the breadcrumbs, the parsley, garlic, and salt. Spoon the mixture into the jalapeño halves. Gently press the stuffed jalapeños in the remaining breadcrumbs. Place the stuffed jalapeños in the prepared basket. Air fry at 188ºC for 20 minutes, or until the cheese is melted and the breadcrumbs are crisp and golden brown.

Shishito Peppers with Herb Dressing

Prep time: 10 minutes | Cook time: 6 minutes | Serves 2 to 4

170 g shishito or Padron peppers
1 tablespoon vegetable oil
Rock salt and freshly ground black pepper, to taste
120 ml mayonnaise
2 tablespoons finely chopped fresh basil leaves
2 tablespoons finely chopped
fresh flat-leaf parsley
1 tablespoon finely chopped fresh tarragon
1 tablespoon finely chopped fresh chives
Finely grated zest of ½ lemon
1 tablespoon fresh lemon juice
Flaky sea salt, for serving

Preheat the air fryer to 204ºC. In a bowl, toss together the shishitos and oil to evenly coat and season with rock salt and black pepper. Transfer to the air fryer and air fry for 6 minutes, shaking the basket halfway through, or until the shishitos are blistered and lightly charred. Meanwhile, in a small bowl, whisk together the mayonnaise, basil, parsley, tarragon, chives, lemon zest, and lemon juice. Pile the peppers on a plate, sprinkle with flaky sea salt, and serve hot with the dressing.

Spicy Chicken Bites

Prep time: 10 minutes | Cook time: 10 to 12 minutes | Makes 30 bites

227 g boneless and skinless chicken thighs, cut into 30 pieces
¼ teaspoon rock salt
2 tablespoons hot sauce
Cooking spray

Preheat the air fryer to 200ºC. Spray the air fryer basket with cooking spray and season the chicken bites with the rock salt, then place in the basket and air fry for 10 to 12 minutes or until crispy. While the chicken bites cook, pour the hot sauce into a large bowl. Remove the bites and add to the sauce bowl, tossing to coat. Serve warm.

Red Pepper Tapenade

Prep time: 5 minutes | Cook time: 5 minutes | Serves 4

1 large red pepper
2 tablespoons plus 1 teaspoon olive oil, divided
120 ml Kalamata olives, pitted
and roughly chopped
1 garlic clove, minced
½ teaspoon dried oregano
1 tablespoon lemon juice

Preheat the air fryer to 192°C. Brush the outside of a whole red pepper with 1 teaspoon olive oil and place it inside the air fryer basket. Roast for 5 minutes. Meanwhile, in a medium bowl combine the remaining 2 tablespoons of olive oil with the olives, garlic, oregano, and lemon juice. Remove the red pepper from the air fryer, then gently slice off the stem and remove the seeds. Roughly chop the roasted pepper into small pieces. Add the red pepper to the olive mixture and stir all together until combined. Serve with pitta chips, crackers, or crusty bread.

Goat Cheese and Garlic Crostini

Prep time: 3 minutes | Cook time: 5 minutes | Serves 4

1 wholemeal baguette
60 ml olive oil
2 garlic cloves, minced
113 g goat cheese
2 tablespoons fresh basil, minced

Preheat the air fryer to 192°C. Cut the baguette into ½-inch-thick slices. In a small bowl, mix together the olive oil and garlic, then brush it over one side of each slice of bread. Place the olive-oil-coated bread in a single layer in the air fryer basket and bake for 5 minutes. Meanwhile, in a small bowl, mix together the goat cheese and basil. Remove the toast from the air fryer, then spread a thin layer of the goat cheese mixture over the top of each piece and serve.

Feta and Quinoa Stuffed Mushrooms

Prep time: 5 minutes | Cook time: 8 minutes | Serves 6

2 tablespoons finely diced red pepper
1 garlic clove, minced
60 ml cooked quinoa
⅛ teaspoon salt
¼ teaspoon dried oregano
24 button mushrooms, stemmed
57 g crumbled feta
3 tablespoons wholemeal breadcrumbs
Olive oil cooking spray

Preheat the air fryer to 182°C. In a small bowl, combine the pepper, garlic, quinoa, salt, and oregano. Spoon the quinoa stuffing into the mushroom caps until just filled. Add a small piece of feta to the top of each mushroom. Sprinkle a pinch breadcrumbs over the feta on each mushroom. Spray the basket of the air fryer with olive oil cooking spray, then gently place the mushrooms into the basket, making sure that they don't touch each other. (Depending on the size of the air fryer, you may have to cook them in two batches.) Place the basket into the air fryer and bake for 8 minutes. Remove from the air fryer and serve.

Greek Yoghurt Devilled Eggs

Prep time: 15 minutes | Cook time: 15 minutes | Serves 4

4 eggs
60 ml non-fat plain Greek yoghurt
1 teaspoon chopped fresh dill
⅛ teaspoon salt
⅛ teaspoon paprika
⅛ teaspoon garlic powder
Chopped fresh parsley, for garnish

Preheat the air fryer to 127°C. Place the eggs in a single layer in the air fryer basket and cook for 15 minutes. Quickly remove the eggs from the air fryer and place them into a cold water bath. Let the eggs cool in the water for 10 minutes before removing and peeling them. After peeling the eggs, cut them in half. Spoon the yolk into a small bowl. Add the yoghurt, dill, salt, paprika, and garlic powder and mix until smooth. Spoon or pipe the yolk mixture into the halved egg whites. Serve with a sprinkle of fresh parsley on top.

Tortellini with Spicy Dipping Sauce

Prep time: 5 minutes | Cook time: 20 minutes | Serves 4

177 ml mayonnaise
2 tablespoons mustard
1 egg
120 ml flour
½ teaspoon dried oregano
355 ml breadcrumbs
2 tablespoons olive oil
475 ml frozen cheese tortellini

Preheat the air fryer to 192°C. In a small bowl, combine the mayonnaise and mustard and mix well. Set aside. In a shallow bowl, beat the egg. In a separate bowl, combine the flour and oregano. In another bowl, combine the breadcrumbs and olive oil, and mix well. Drop the tortellini, a few at a time, into the egg, then into the flour, then into the egg again, and then into the breadcrumbs to coat. Put into the air fryer basket, cooking in batches. Air fry for about 10 minutes, shaking halfway through the cooking time, or until the tortellini are crisp and golden brown on the outside. Serve with the mayonnaise mixture.

Sea Salt Potato Crisps

Prep time: 30 minutes | Cook time: 27 minutes | Serves 4

Oil, for spraying
4 medium yellow potatoes such as Maris Pipers
1 tablespoon oil
⅛ to ¼ teaspoon fine sea salt

Line the air fryer basket with parchment and spray lightly with oil. Using a mandoline or a very sharp knife, cut the potatoes into very thin slices. Place the slices in a bowl of cold water and let soak for about 20 minutes. Drain the potatoes, transfer them to a plate lined with paper towels, and pat dry. Drizzle the oil over the potatoes, sprinkle with the salt, and toss to combine. Transfer to the prepared basket. Air fry at 92°C for 20 minutes. Toss the crisps, increase the heat to 204°C, and cook for another 5 to 7 minutes, until crispy.

Polenta Fries with Chilli-Lime Mayo

Prep time: 10 minutes | Cook time: 28 minutes | Serves 4

Polenta Fries:
2 teaspoons vegetable or olive oil
¼ teaspoon paprika
450 g prepared polenta, cut into 3-inch × ½-inch strips
Chilli-Lime Mayo:
120 ml mayonnaise

1 teaspoon chilli powder
1 teaspoon chopped fresh coriander
¼ teaspoon ground cumin
Juice of ½ lime
Salt and freshly ground black pepper, to taste

Preheat the air fryer to 204°C. Mix the oil and paprika in a bowl. Add the polenta strips and toss until evenly coated. Transfer the polenta strips to the air fry basket and air fry for 28 minutes until the fries are golden brown, shaking the basket once during cooking. Season as desired with salt and pepper. Meanwhile, whisk together all the ingredients for the chilli-lime mayo in a small bowl. Remove the polenta fries from the air fryer to a plate and serve alongside the chilli-lime mayo as a dipping sauce.

Golden Onion Rings

Prep time: 15 minutes | Cook time: 14 minutes per batch | Serves 4

1 large white onion, peeled and cut into ½ to ¾-inch-thick slices (about 475 ml)
120 ml semi-skimmed milk
240 ml wholemeal pastry flour, or plain flour
2 tablespoons cornflour
¾ teaspoon sea salt, divided
½ teaspoon freshly ground black

pepper, divided
¾ teaspoon granulated garlic, divided
355 ml wholemeal breadcrumbs, or gluten-free breadcrumbs
Cooking oil spray (coconut, sunflower, or safflower)
Ketchup, for serving (optional)

Carefully separate the onion slices into rings—a gentle touch is important here. Place the milk in a shallow bowl and set aside. Make the first breading: In a medium bowl, stir together the flour, cornflour, ¼ teaspoon of salt, ¼ teaspoon of pepper, and ¼ teaspoon of granulated garlic. Set aside. Make the second breading: In a separate medium bowl, stir together the breadcrumbs with the remaining ½ teaspoon of salt, the remaining ½ teaspoon of garlic, and the remaining ½ teaspoon of pepper. Set aside. Insert the crisper plate into the basket and the basket into the unit. Preheat the unit by selecting AIR FRY, setting the temperature to 200°C, and setting the time to 3 minutes. Select START/STOP to begin. Once the unit is preheated, spray the crisper plate and the basket with cooking oil. To make the onion rings, dip one ring into the milk and into the first breading mixture. Dip the ring into the milk again and back into the first breading mixture, coating thoroughly. Dip the ring into the milk one last time and then into the second breading mixture, coating thoroughly. Gently lay the onion ring in the basket. Repeat with additional rings and, as you place them into the basket, do not overlap them too much. Once all the onion rings are in the basket, generously spray the tops with cooking oil. Select AIR FRY, set the temperature to 200°C, and set the time to 14 minutes. Insert the basket into the unit. Select START/STOP to begin. After 4 minutes, open the unit and spray the rings generously with cooking

oil. Close the unit to resume cooking. After 3 minutes, remove the basket and spray the onion rings again. Remove the rings, turn them over, and place them back into the basket. Generously spray them again with oil. Reinsert the basket to resume cooking. After 4 minutes, generously spray the rings with oil one last time. Resume cooking for the remaining 3 minutes, or until the onion rings are very crunchy and brown. 1When the cooking is complete, serve the hot rings with ketchup, or other sauce of choice.

Cheese-Stuffed Blooming Onion

Prep time: 10 minutes | Cook time: 15 minutes | Serves 2

1 large brown onion (397 g)
1 tablespoon olive oil
Rock salt and freshly ground black pepper, to taste
60 ml plus 2 tablespoons panko breadcrumbs
60 ml grated Parmesan cheese

3 tablespoons mayonnaise
1 tablespoon fresh lemon juice
1 tablespoon chopped fresh flat-leaf parsley
2 teaspoons whole-grain Dijon mustard
1 garlic clove, minced

Place the onion on a cutting board and trim the top off and peel off the outer skin. Turn the onion upside down and use a paring knife, cut vertical slits halfway through the onion at ½-inch intervals around the onion, keeping the root intact. When you turn the onion right side up, it should open up like the petals of a flower. Drizzle the cut sides of the onion with the olive oil and season with salt and pepper. Place petal-side up in the air fryer and air fry at 176°C for 10 minutes. Meanwhile, in a bowl, stir together the panko, Parmesan, mayonnaise, lemon juice, parsley, mustard, and garlic until incorporated into a smooth paste. Remove the onion from the fryer and stuff the paste all over and in between the onion "petals." Return the onion to the air fryer and air fry at 192°C until the onion is tender in the centre and the bread crumb mixture is golden brown, about 5 minutes. Remove the onion from the air fryer, transfer to a plate, and serve hot.

Fried Artichoke Hearts

Prep time: 10 minutes | Cook time: 12 minutes | Serves 10

Oil, for spraying
3 (397 g) cans quartered artichokes, drained and patted dry
120 ml mayonnaise

240 ml panko breadcrumbs
80 ml grated Parmesan cheese
Salt and freshly ground black pepper, to taste

Line the air fryer basket with parchment and spray lightly with oil. Place the artichokes on a plate. Put the mayonnaise and breadcrumbs in separate bowls. Working one at a time, dredge each artichoke piece in the mayonnaise, then in the breadcrumbs to cover. Place the artichokes in the prepared basket. You may need to work in batches, depending on the size of your air fryer. Air fry at 188°C for 10 to 12 minutes, or until crispy and golden brown. Sprinkle with the Parmesan cheese and season with salt and black pepper. Serve immediately.

Onion Pakoras

Prep time: 30 minutes | Cook time: 10 minutes per batch | Serves 2

2 medium brown or white onions, sliced (475 ml)
120 ml chopped fresh coriander
2 tablespoons vegetable oil
1 tablespoon chickpea flour
1 tablespoon rice flour, or 2

tablespoons chickpea flour
1 teaspoon ground turmeric
1 teaspoon cumin seeds
1 teaspoon rock salt
½ teaspoon cayenne pepper
Vegetable oil spray

In a large bowl, combine the onions, coriander, oil, chickpea flour, rice flour, turmeric, cumin seeds, salt, and cayenne. Stir to combine. Cover and let stand for 30 minutes or up to overnight. (This allows the onions to release moisture, creating a batter.) Mix well before using. Spray the air fryer basket generously with vegetable oil spray. Drop half of the batter in 6 heaping tablespoons into the basket. Set the air fryer to 176°C for 8 minutes. Carefully turn the pakoras over and spray with oil spray. Set the air fryer for 2 minutes, or until the batter is cooked through and crisp. Repeat with remaining batter to make 6 more pakoras, checking at 6 minutes for doneness. Serve hot.

Veggie Shrimp Toast

Prep time: 15 minutes | Cook time: 3 to 6 minutes | Serves 4

8 large raw shrimp, peeled and finely chopped
1 egg white
2 garlic cloves, minced
3 tablespoons minced red pepper

1 medium celery stalk, minced
2 tablespoons cornflour
¼ teaspoon Chinese five-spice powder
3 slices firm thin-sliced no-salt wholemeal bread

Preheat the air fryer to 176°C. In a small bowl, stir together the shrimp, egg white, garlic, red pepper, celery, cornflour, and five-spice powder. Top each slice of bread with one-third of the shrimp mixture, spreading it evenly to the edges. With a sharp knife, cut each slice of bread into 4 strips. Place the shrimp toasts in the air fryer basket in a single layer. You may need to cook them in batches. Air fry for 3 to 6 minutes, until crisp and golden brown. Serve hot.

Shrimp Pirogues

Prep time: 15 minutes | Cook time: 4 to 5 minutes | Serves 8

340 g small, peeled, and deveined raw shrimp
85 g soft white cheese, room temperature
2 tablespoons natural yoghurt
1 teaspoon lemon juice

1 teaspoon dried dill weed, crushed
Salt, to taste
4 small hothouse cucumbers, each approximately 6 inches long

Pour 4 tablespoons water in bottom of air fryer drawer. Place shrimp in air fryer basket in single layer and air fry at 200°C for 4 to 5 minutes, just until done. Watch carefully because shrimp cooks quickly, and overcooking makes it tough. Chop shrimp into small pieces, no larger than ½ inch. Refrigerate while mixing the remaining ingredients. With a fork, mash and whip the soft white cheese until smooth. Stir in the yoghurt and beat until smooth. Stir in lemon juice, dill weed, and chopped shrimp. Taste for seasoning. If needed, add ¼ to ½ teaspoon salt to suit your taste. Store in refrigerator until serving time. When ready to serve, wash and dry cucumbers and split them lengthwise. Scoop out the seeds and turn cucumbers upside down on paper towels to drain for 10 minutes. Just before filling, wipe centres of cucumbers dry. Spoon the shrimp mixture into the pirogues and cut in half crosswise. Serve immediately.

Lemon-Pepper Chicken Drumsticks

Prep time: 30 minutes | Cook time: 30 minutes | Serves 2

2 teaspoons freshly ground coarse black pepper
1 teaspoon baking powder
½ teaspoon garlic powder

4 chicken drumsticks (113 g each)
Rock salt, to taste
1 lemon

In a small bowl, stir together the pepper, baking powder, and garlic powder. Place the drumsticks on a plate and sprinkle evenly with the baking powder mixture, turning the drumsticks so they're well coated. Let the drumsticks stand in the refrigerator for at least 1 hour or up to overnight. Sprinkle the drumsticks with salt, then transfer them to the air fryer, standing them bone-end up and leaning against the wall of the air fryer basket. Air fry at 192°C until cooked through and crisp on the outside, about 30 minutes. Transfer the drumsticks to a serving platter and finely grate the zest of the lemon over them while they're hot. Cut the lemon into wedges and serve with the warm drumsticks.

Sweet Potato Fries with Mayonnaise

Prep time: 5 minutes | Cook time: 20 minutes | Serves 2 to 3

1 large sweet potato (about 450 g), scrubbed
1 teaspoon vegetable or rapeseed oil
Salt, to taste
Dipping Sauce:

60 ml light mayonnaise
½ teaspoon sriracha sauce
1 tablespoon spicy brown mustard
1 tablespoon sweet Thai chilli sauce

Preheat the air fryer to 92°C. On a flat work surface, cut the sweet potato into fry-shaped strips about ¼ inch wide and ¼ inch thick. You can use a mandoline to slice the sweet potato quickly and uniformly. In a medium bowl, drizzle the sweet potato strips with the oil and toss well. Transfer to the air fryer basket and air fry for 10 minutes, shaking the basket twice during cooking. Remove the air fryer basket and sprinkle with the salt and toss to coat. Increase the air fryer temperature to 204°C and air fry for an additional 10 minutes, or until the fries are crispy and tender. Shake the basket a few times during cooking. Meanwhile, whisk together all the ingredients for the sauce in a small bowl. Remove the sweet potato fries from the basket to a plate and serve warm alongside the dipping sauce.

Kale Chips with Tex-Mex Dip

Prep time: 10 minutes | Cook time: 5 to 6 minutes | Serves 8

240 ml Greek yoghurt
1 tablespoon chilli powder
80 ml low-salt salsa, well drained

1 bunch curly kale
1 teaspoon olive oil
¼ teaspoon coarse sea salt

In a small bowl, combine the yoghurt, chilli powder, and drained salsa; refrigerate. Rinse the kale thoroughly, and pat dry. Remove the stems and ribs from the kale, using a sharp knife. Cut or tear the leaves into 3-inch pieces. Toss the kale with the olive oil in a large bowl. Air fry the kale in small batches at 200°C until the leaves are crisp. This should take 5 to 6 minutes. Shake the basket once during cooking time. As you remove the kale chips, sprinkle them with a bit of the sea salt. When all of the kale chips are done, serve with the dip.

Beef and Mango Skewers

Prep time: 10 minutes | Cook time: 4 to 7 minutes | Serves 4

340 g beef sirloin tip, cut into 1-inch cubes
2 tablespoons balsamic vinegar
1 tablespoon olive oil
1 tablespoon honey

½ teaspoon dried marjoram
Pinch of salt
Freshly ground black pepper, to taste
1 mango

Preheat the air fryer to 200°C. Put the beef cubes in a medium bowl and add the balsamic vinegar, olive oil, honey, marjoram, salt, and pepper. Mix well, then massage the marinade into the beef with your hands. Set aside. To prepare the mango, stand it on end and cut the skin off, using a sharp knife. Then carefully cut around the oval pit to remove the flesh. Cut the mango into 1-inch cubes. Thread metal skewers alternating with three beef cubes and two mango cubes. Roast the skewers in the air fryer basket for 4 to 7 minutes, or until the beef is browned and at least 63°C. Serve hot.

Ranch Oyster Snack Crackers

Prep time: 3 minutes | Cook time: 12 minutes | Serves 6

Oil, for spraying
60 ml olive oil
2 teaspoons dry ranch seasoning
1 teaspoon chilli powder
½ teaspoon dried dill

½ teaspoon granulated garlic
½ teaspoon salt
1 (255 g) bag oyster crackers or low-salt crackers

Preheat the air fryer to 164°C. Line the air fryer basket with parchment and spray lightly with oil. In a large bowl, mix together the olive oil, ranch seasoning, chilli powder, dill, garlic, and salt. Add the crackers and toss until evenly coated. Place the mixture in the prepared basket. Cook for 10 to 12 minutes, shaking or stirring every 3 to 4 minutes, or until crisp and golden brown.

Root Veggie Chips with Herb Salt

Prep time: 10 minutes | Cook time: 8 minutes | Serves 2

1 parsnip, washed
1 small beetroot, washed
1 small turnip, washed
½ small sweet potato, washed
1 teaspoon olive oil

Cooking spray
Herb Salt:
¼ teaspoon rock salt
2 teaspoons finely chopped fresh parsley

Preheat the air fryer to 182°C. Peel and thinly slice the parsnip, beetroot, turnip, and sweet potato, then place the vegetables in a large bowl, add the olive oil, and toss. Spray the air fryer basket with cooking spray, then place the vegetables in the basket and air fry for 8 minutes, gently shaking the basket halfway through. While the chips cook, make the herb salt in a small bowl by combining the rock salt and parsley. Remove the chips and place on a serving plate, then sprinkle the herb salt on top and allow to cool for 2 to 3 minutes before serving.

Rosemary-Garlic Shoestring Fries

Prep time: 5 minutes | Cook time: 18 minutes | Serves 2

1 large russet or Maris Piper potato (about 340 g), scrubbed clean, and julienned
1 tablespoon vegetable oil
Leaves from 1 sprig fresh

rosemary
Rock salt and freshly ground black pepper, to taste
1 garlic clove, thinly sliced
Flaky sea salt, for serving

Preheat the air fryer to 204°C. Place the julienned potatoes in a large colander and rinse under cold running water until the water runs clear. Spread the potatoes out on a double-thick layer of paper towels and pat dry. In a large bowl, combine the potatoes, oil, and rosemary. Season with rock salt and pepper and toss to coat evenly. Place the potatoes in the air fryer and air fry for 18 minutes, shaking the basket every 5 minutes and adding the garlic in the last 5 minutes of cooking, or until the fries are golden brown and crisp. Transfer the fries to a plate and sprinkle with flaky sea salt while they're hot. Serve immediately.

Chapter 3 Breakfasts

Chapter 3 Breakfasts

Savory Sweet Potato Hash

Prep time: 15 minutes | Cook time: 18 minutes | Serves 6

2 medium sweet potatoes, peeled and cut into 1-inch cubes
½ green pepper, diced
½ red onion, diced
110 g baby mushrooms, diced
2 tablespoons olive oil
1 garlic clove, minced
½ teaspoon salt
½ teaspoon black pepper
½ tablespoon chopped fresh rosemary

Preheat the air fryer to 192°C. In a large bowl, toss all ingredients together until the vegetables are well coated and seasonings distributed. Pour the vegetables into the air fryer basket, making sure they are in a single even layer. (If using a smaller air fryer, you may need to do this in two batches.) Roast for 9 minutes, then toss or flip the vegetables. Roast for 9 minutes more. Transfer to a serving bowl or individual plates and enjoy.

Broccoli-Mushroom Frittata

Prep time: 10 minutes | Cook time: 20 minutes | Serves 2

1 tablespoon olive oil
350 ml broccoli florets, finely chopped
120 ml sliced brown mushrooms
60 ml finely chopped onion
½ teaspoon salt
¼ teaspoon freshly ground black pepper
6 eggs
60 ml Parmesan cheese

In a nonstick cake pan, combine the olive oil, broccoli, mushrooms, onion, salt, and pepper. Stir until the vegetables are thoroughly coated with oil. Place the cake pan in the air fryer basket and set the air fryer to 204°C. Air fry for 5 minutes until the vegetables soften. Meanwhile, in a medium bowl, whisk the eggs and Parmesan until thoroughly combined. Pour the egg mixture into the pan and shake gently to distribute the vegetables. Air fry for another 15 minutes until the eggs are set. Remove from the air fryer and let sit for 5 minutes to cool slightly. Use a silicone spatula to gently lift the frittata onto a plate before serving.

White Bean–Oat Waffles

Prep time: 10 minutes | Cook time: 20 minutes | Serves 2

1 large egg white
2 tablespoons finely ground flaxseed
120 ml water
¼ teaspoon salt
1 teaspoon vanilla extract
120 ml cannellini beans, drained and rinsed
1 teaspoon coconut oil
1 teaspoon liquid sweetener
120 ml old-fashioned rolled oats
Extra-virgin olive oil cooking spray

In a blender, combine the egg white, flaxseed, water, salt, vanilla, cannellini beans, coconut oil, and sweetener. Blend on high for 90 seconds. Add the oats. Blend for 1 minute more. Preheat the waffle iron. The batter will thicken to the correct consistency while the waffle iron preheats. Spray the heated waffle iron with cooking spray. Add 180 ml batter. Close the waffle iron. Cook for 6 to 8 minutes, or until done. Repeated with the remaining batter. Serve hot, with your favorite sugar-free topping.

Turkey Breakfast Sausage Patties

Prep time: 5 minutes | Cook time: 10 minutes | Serves 4

1 tablespoon chopped fresh thyme
1 tablespoon chopped fresh sage
1¼ teaspoons coarse or flaky salt
1 teaspoon chopped fennel seeds
¾ teaspoon smoked paprika
½ teaspoon onion granules
½ teaspoon garlic powder
⅛ teaspoon crushed red pepper flakes
⅛ teaspoon freshly ground black pepper
450 g lean turkey mince
120 ml finely minced sweet apple (peeled)

Thoroughly combine the thyme, sage, salt, fennel seeds, paprika, onion granules, garlic powder, red pepper flakes, and black pepper in a medium bowl. Add the turkey mince and apple and stir until well incorporated. Divide the mixture into 8 equal portions and shape into patties with your hands, each about ¼ inch thick and 3 inches in diameter. Preheat the air fryer to 204°C. Place the patties in the air fryer basket in a single layer. You may need to work in batches to avoid overcrowding. Air fry for 5 minutes. Flip the patties and air fry for 5 minutes, or until the patties are nicely browned and cooked through. Remove from the basket to a plate and repeat with the remaining patties. Serve warm.

Breakfast Meatballs

Prep time: 10 minutes | Cook time: 15 minutes | Makes 18 meatballs

450 g pork sausage meat, removed from casings
½ teaspoon salt
¼ teaspoon ground black pepper
120 ml shredded sharp Cheddar cheese
30 g cream cheese, softened
1 large egg, whisked

Combine all ingredients in a large bowl. Form mixture into eighteen 1-inch meatballs. Place meatballs into ungreased air fryer basket. Adjust the temperature to 204°C and air fry for 15 minutes, shaking basket three times during cooking. Meatballs will be browned on the outside and have an internal temperature of at least 64°C when completely cooked. Serve warm.

Cheddar Soufflés

Prep time: 15 minutes | Cook time: 12 minutes | Serves 4

3 large eggs, whites and yolks separated
¼ teaspoon cream of tartar
120 ml shredded sharp Cheddar cheese
85 g cream cheese, softened

In a large bowl, beat egg whites together with cream of tartar until soft peaks form, about 2 minutes. In a separate medium bowl, beat egg yolks, Cheddar, and cream cheese together until frothy, about 1 minute. Add egg yolk mixture to whites, gently folding until combined. Pour mixture evenly into four ramekins greased with cooking spray. Place ramekins into air fryer basket. Adjust the temperature to 176ºC and bake for 12 minutes. Eggs will be browned on the top and firm in the center when done. Serve warm.

Gluten-Free Granola Cereal

Prep time: 7 minutes | Cook time: 30 minutes | Makes 820 ml

Oil, for spraying
350 ml gluten-free rolled oats
120 ml chopped walnuts
120 ml chopped almonds
120 ml pumpkin seeds
60 ml maple syrup or honey
1 tablespoon toasted sesame oil or vegetable oil
1 teaspoon ground cinnamon
½ teaspoon salt
120 ml dried cranberries

Preheat the air fryer to 120ºC. Line the air fryer basket with parchment and spray lightly with oil. (Do not skip the step of lining the basket; the parchment will keep the granola from falling through the holes.) In a large bowl, mix together the oats, walnuts, almonds, pumpkin seeds, maple syrup, sesame oil, cinnamon, and salt. Spread the mixture in an even layer in the prepared basket. Cook for 30 minutes, stirring every 10 minutes. Transfer the granola to a bowl, add the dried cranberries, and toss to combine. Let cool to room temperature before storing in an airtight container.

Mississippi Spice Muffins

Prep time: 15 minutes | Cook time: 13 minutes | Makes 12 muffins

1 L plain flour
1 tablespoon ground cinnamon
2 teaspoons baking soda
2 teaspoons allspice
1 teaspoon ground cloves
1 teaspoon salt
235 ml (2 sticks) butter, room
temperature
475 ml sugar
2 large eggs, lightly beaten
475 ml unsweetened applesauce
60 ml chopped pecans
1 to 2 tablespoons oil

In a large bowl, whisk the flour, cinnamon, baking soda, allspice, cloves, and salt until blended. In another large bowl, combine the butter and sugar. Using an electric mixer, beat the mixture for 2 to 3 minutes until light and fluffy. Add the beaten eggs and stir until blended. Add the flour mixture and applesauce, alternating between the two and blending after each addition. Stir in the pecans. Preheat the air fryer to 164ºC. Spritz 12 silicone muffin cups with oil. Pour the batter into the prepared muffin cups, filling each halfway. Place the muffins in the air fryer basket. Air fry for 6 minutes. Shake the basket and air fry for 7 minutes more. The muffins are done when a toothpick inserted into the middle comes out clean.

Apple Rolls

Prep time: 20 minutes | Cook time: 20 to 24 minutes | Makes 12 rolls

Apple Rolls:
475 ml plain flour, plus more for dusting
2 tablespoons granulated sugar
1 teaspoon salt
3 tablespoons butter, at room temperature
180 ml milk, whole or semi-skimmed
120 ml packed light brown
sugar
1 teaspoon ground cinnamon
1 large Granny Smith apple, peeled and diced
1 to 2 tablespoons oil
Icing:
120 ml icing sugar
½ teaspoon vanilla extract
2 to 3 tablespoons milk, whole or semi-skimmed

Make the Apple Rolls In a large bowl, whisk the flour, granulated sugar, and salt until blended. Stir in the butter and milk briefly until a sticky dough forms. In a small bowl, stir together the brown sugar, cinnamon, and apple. Place a piece of parchment paper on a work surface and dust it with flour. Roll the dough on the prepared surface to ¼ inch thickness. Spread the apple mixture over the dough. Roll up the dough jelly roll-style, pinching the ends to seal. Cut the dough into 12 rolls. Preheat the air fryer to 160ºC. Line the air fryer basket with parchment paper and spritz it with oil. Place 6 rolls on the prepared parchment. Bake for 5 minutes. Flip the rolls and bake for 5 to 7 minutes more until lightly browned. Repeat with the remaining rolls. Make the Icing In a medium bowl, whisk the icing sugar, vanilla, and milk until blended. Drizzle over the warm rolls.

Egg Tarts

Prep time: 10 minutes | Cook time: 17 to 20 minutes | Makes 2 tarts

⅓ sheet frozen puff pastry, thawed
Cooking oil spray
120 ml shredded Cheddar cheese
2 eggs
¼ teaspoon salt, divided
1 teaspoon minced fresh parsley (optional)

Insert the crisper plate into the basket and the basket into the unit. Preheat the unit by selecting BAKE, setting the temperature to 200ºC, and setting the time to 3 minutes. Select START/STOP to begin. Lay the puff pastry sheet on a piece of parchment paper and cut it in half. Once the unit is preheated, spray the crisper plate with cooking oil. Transfer the 2 squares of pastry to the basket, keeping them on the parchment paper. Select BAKE, set the temperature to 200ºC, and set the time to 20 minutes. Select START/STOP to begin. After 10 minutes, use a metal spoon to press down the center of each pastry square to make a well. Divide the cheese equally between the baked pastries. Carefully crack an egg on top of the cheese, and sprinkle each with the salt. Resume cooking for 7 to 10 minutes. When the cooking is complete, the eggs will be cooked through. Sprinkle each with parsley (if using) and serve.

Portobello Eggs Benedict

Prep time: 10 minutes | Cook time: 10 to 14 minutes | Serves 2

1 tablespoon olive oil
2 cloves garlic, minced
¼ teaspoon dried thyme
2 portobello mushrooms, stems removed and gills scraped out
2 plum tomatoes, halved lengthwise
Salt and freshly ground black

pepper, to taste
2 large eggs
2 tablespoons grated Pecorino Romano cheese
1 tablespoon chopped fresh parsley, for garnish
1 teaspoon truffle oil (optional)

Preheat the air fryer to 204ºC. In a small bowl, combine the olive oil, garlic, and thyme. Brush the mixture over the mushrooms and tomatoes until thoroughly coated. Season to taste with salt and freshly ground black pepper. Arrange the vegetables, cut side up, in the air fryer basket. Crack an egg into the center of each mushroom and sprinkle with cheese. Air fry for 10 to 14 minutes until the vegetables are tender and the whites are firm. When cool enough to handle, coarsely chop the tomatoes and place on top of the eggs. Scatter parsley on top and drizzle with truffle oil, if desired, just before serving.

Jalapeño Popper Egg Cups

Prep time: 10 minutes | Cook time: 10 minutes | Serves 2

4 large eggs
60 ml chopped pickled jalapeños
60 g full-fat cream cheese

120 ml shredded sharp Cheddar cheese

In a medium bowl, beat the eggs, then pour into four silicone muffin cups. In a large microwave-safe bowl, place jalapeños, cream cheese, and Cheddar. Microwave for 30 seconds and stir. Take a spoonful, approximately ¼ of the mixture, and place it in the center of one of the egg cups. Repeat with remaining mixture. Place egg cups into the air fryer basket. Adjust the temperature to 160ºC and bake for 10 minutes. Serve warm.

Spinach and Mushroom Mini Quiche

Prep time: 10 minutes | Cook time: 15 minutes | Serves 4

1 teaspoon olive oil, plus more for spraying
235 ml coarsely chopped mushrooms
235 ml fresh baby spinach, shredded
4 eggs, beaten

120 ml shredded Cheddar cheese
120 ml shredded Mozzarella cheese
¼ teaspoon salt
¼ teaspoon black pepper

Spray 4 silicone baking cups with olive oil and set aside. In a medium sauté pan over medium heat, warm 1 teaspoon of olive oil. Add the mushrooms and sauté until soft, 3 to 4 minutes. Add the spinach and cook until wilted, 1 to 2 minutes. Set aside. In a medium bowl, whisk together the eggs, Cheddar cheese, Mozzarella cheese, salt, and pepper. Gently fold the mushrooms and spinach into the egg mixture. Pour ¼ of the mixture into each silicone baking cup. Place the baking cups into the air fryer basket and air fry at 176ºC for 5 minutes. Stir the mixture in each ramekin slightly and air fry until the egg has set, an additional 3 to 5 minutes.

Mushroom-and-Tomato Stuffed Hash Browns

Prep time: 10 minutes | Cook time: 20 minutes | Serves 4

Olive oil cooking spray
1 tablespoon plus 2 teaspoons olive oil, divided
110 g baby mushrooms, diced
1 spring onion, white parts and green parts, diced

1 garlic clove, minced
475 ml shredded potatoes
½ teaspoon salt
¼ teaspoon black pepper
1 plum tomato, diced
120 ml shredded mozzarella

Preheat the air fryer to 192ºC. Lightly coat the inside of a 6-inch cake pan with olive oil cooking spray. In a small skillet, heat 2 teaspoons olive oil over medium heat. Add the mushrooms, spring onion, and garlic, and cook for 4 to 5 minutes, or until they have softened and are beginning to show some color. Remove from heat. Meanwhile, in a large bowl, combine the potatoes, salt, pepper, and the remaining tablespoon olive oil. Toss until all potatoes are well coated. Pour half of the potatoes into the bottom of the cake pan. Top with the mushroom mixture, tomato, and mozzarella. Spread the remaining potatoes over the top. Bake in the air fryer for 12 to 15 minutes, or until the top is golden brown. Remove from the air fryer and allow to cool for 5 minutes before slicing and serving.

Homemade Cherry Breakfast Tarts

Prep time: 15 minutes | Cook time: 20 minutes | Serves 6

Tarts:
2 refrigerated piecrusts
80 ml cherry preserves
1 teaspoon cornflour
Cooking oil

Frosting:
120 ml vanilla yoghurt
30 g cream cheese
1 teaspoon stevia
Rainbow sprinkles

Make the Tarts Place the piecrusts on a flat surface. Using a knife or pizza cutter, cut each piecrust into 3 rectangles, for 6 total. (I discard the unused dough left from slicing the edges.) In a small bowl, combine the preserves and cornflour. Mix well. Scoop 1 tablespoon of the preserves mixture onto the top half of each piece of piecrust. Fold the bottom of each piece up to close the tart. Using the back of a fork, press along the edges of each tart to seal. Spray the breakfast tarts with cooking oil and place them in the air fryer. I do not recommend stacking the breakfast tarts. They will stick together if stacked. You may need to prepare them in two batches. Bake at 375ºF for 10 minutes. Allow the breakfast tarts to cool fully before removing from the air fryer. If necessary, repeat steps 5 and 6 for the remaining breakfast tarts. Make the Frosting In a small bowl, combine the yoghurt, cream cheese, and stevia. Mix well. Spread the breakfast tarts with frosting and top with sprinkles, and serve.

Mexican Breakfast Pepper Rings

Prep time: 5 minutes | Cook time: 10 minutes | Serves 4

Olive oil
1 large red, yellow, or orange pepper, cut into four ¾-inch rings

4 eggs
Salt and freshly ground black pepper, to taste
2 teaspoons salsa

Preheat the air fryer to 176ºC. Lightly spray a baking pan with olive oil. Place 2 bell pepper rings on the pan. Crack one egg into each bell pepper ring. Season with salt and black pepper. Spoon ½ teaspoon of salsa on top of each egg. Place the pan in the air fryer basket. Air fry until the yolk is slightly runny, 5 to 6 minutes or until the yolk is fully cooked, 8 to 10 minutes. Repeat with the remaining 2 pepper rings. Serve hot.

Homemade Toaster Pastries

Prep time: 10 minutes | Cook time: 11 minutes | Makes 6 pastries

Oil, for spraying
1 (425 g) package refrigerated piecrust
6 tablespoons jam or preserves of choice

475 ml icing sugar
3 tablespoons milk
1 to 2 tablespoons sprinkles of choice

Preheat the air fryer to 176ºC. Line the air fryer basket with parchment and spray lightly with oil. Cut the piecrust into 12 rectangles, about 3 by 4 inches each. You will need to reroll the dough scraps to get 12 rectangles. Spread 1 tablespoon of jam in the center of 6 rectangles, leaving ¼ inch around the edges. Pour some water into a small bowl. Use your finger to moisten the edge of each rectangle. Top each rectangle with another and use your fingers to press around the edges. Using the tines of a fork, seal the edges of the dough and poke a few holes in the top of each one. Place the pastries in the prepared basket. Air fry for 11 minutes. Let cool completely. In a medium bowl, whisk together the icing sugar and milk. Spread the icing over the tops of the pastries and add sprinkles. Serve immediately.

Southwestern Ham Egg Cups

Prep time: 5 minutes | Cook time: 12 minutes | Serves 2

4 (30 g) slices wafer-thin ham
4 large eggs
2 tablespoons full-fat sour cream
60 ml diced green pepper

2 tablespoons diced red pepper
2 tablespoons diced brown onion
120 ml shredded medium Cheddar cheese

Place one slice of ham on the bottom of four baking cups. In a large bowl, whisk eggs with sour cream. Stir in green pepper, red pepper, and onion. Pour the egg mixture into ham-lined baking cups. Top with Cheddar. Place cups into the air fryer basket. Adjust the temperature to 160ºC and bake for 12 minutes or until the tops are browned. Serve warm.

Golden Avocado Tempura

Prep time: 5 minutes | Cook time: 10 minutes | Serves 4

120 ml bread crumbs
½ teaspoons salt
1 Haas avocado, pitted, peeled

and sliced
Liquid from 1 can white beans

Preheat the air fryer to 176ºC. Mix the bread crumbs and salt in a shallow bowl until well-incorporated. Dip the avocado slices in the bean liquid, then into the bread crumbs. Put the avocados in the air fryer, taking care not to overlap any slices, and air fry for 10 minutes, giving the basket a good shake at the halfway point. Serve immediately.

Cinnamon-Raisin Bagels

Prep time: 30 minutes | Cook time: 10 minutes | Makes 4 bagels

Oil, for spraying
60 ml raisins
235 ml self-raising flour, plus more for dusting

235 ml plain Greek yoghurt
1 teaspoon ground cinnamon
1 large egg

Line the air fryer basket with parchment and spray lightly with oil. Place the raisins in a bowl of hot water and let sit for 10 to 15 minutes, until they have plumped. This will make them extra juicy. In a large bowl, mix together the flour, yoghurt, and cinnamon with your hands or a large silicone spatula until a ball is formed. It will be quite sticky for a while. Drain the raisins and gently work them into the ball of dough. Place the dough on a lightly floured work surface and divide into 4 equal pieces. Roll each piece into an 8- or 9-inch-long rope and shape it into a circle, pinching the ends together to seal. In a small bowl, whisk the egg. Brush the egg onto the tops of the dough. Place the dough in the prepared basket. Air fry at 176ºC for 10 minutes. Serve immediately.

Buffalo Chicken Breakfast Muffins

Prep time: 7 minutes | Cook time: 13 to 16 minutes | Serves 10

170 g shredded cooked chicken
85 g blue cheese, crumbled
2 tablespoons unsalted butter, melted
80 ml Buffalo hot sauce, such as Frank's RedHot

1 teaspoon minced garlic
6 large eggs
Sea salt and freshly ground black pepper, to taste
Avocado oil spray

In a large bowl, stir together the chicken, blue cheese, melted butter, hot sauce, and garlic. In a medium bowl or large liquid measuring cup, beat the eggs. Season with salt and pepper. Spray 10 silicone muffin cups with oil. Divide the chicken mixture among the cups, and pour the egg mixture over top. Place the cups in the air fryer and set to 150ºC. Bake for 13 to 16 minutes, until the muffins are set and cooked through. (Depending on the size of your air fryer, you may need to cook the muffins in batches.)

Egg and Bacon Muffins

Prep time: 5 minutes | Cook time: 15 minutes | Serves 1

2 eggs
Salt and ground black pepper, to taste
1 tablespoon green pesto
85 g shredded Cheddar cheese
140 g cooked bacon
1 spring onion, chopped

Preheat the air fryer to 176°C. Line a cupcake tin with parchment paper. Beat the eggs with pepper, salt, and pesto in a bowl. Mix in the cheese. Pour the eggs into the cupcake tin and top with the bacon and spring onion. Bake in the preheated air fryer for 15 minutes, or until the egg is set. Serve immediately.

Scotch Eggs

Prep time: 10 minutes | Cook time: 20 to 25 minutes | Serves 4

2 tablespoons flour, plus extra for coating
450 g sausage meat
4 hard-boiled eggs, peeled
1 raw egg
1 tablespoon water
Oil for misting or cooking spray
Crumb Coating:
180 ml panko bread crumbs
180 ml flour

Combine flour with sausage meat and mix thoroughly. Divide into 4 equal portions and mold each around a hard-boiled egg so the sausage completely covers the egg. In a small bowl, beat together the raw egg and water. Dip sausage-covered eggs in the remaining flour, then the egg mixture, then roll in the crumb coating. Air fry at 182°C for 10 minutes. Spray eggs, turn, and spray other side. Continue cooking for another 10 to 15 minutes or until sausage is well done.

Wholemeal Banana-Walnut Bread

Prep time: 10 minutes | Cook time: 23 minutes | Serves 6

Olive oil cooking spray
2 ripe medium bananas
1 large egg
60 ml non-fat plain Greek yoghurt
60 ml olive oil
½ teaspoon vanilla extract
2 tablespoons honey
235 ml wholemeal flour
¼ teaspoon salt
¼ teaspoon baking soda
½ teaspoon ground cinnamon
60 ml chopped walnuts

Preheat the air fryer to 182°C. Lightly coat the inside of a 8-by-4-inch loaf pan with olive oil cooking spray. (Or use two 5 ½-by-3-inch loaf pans.) In a large bowl, mash the bananas with a fork. Add the egg, yoghurt, olive oil, vanilla, and honey. Mix until well combined and mostly smooth. Sift the wholemeal flour, salt, baking soda, and cinnamon into the wet mixture, then stir until just combined. Do not overmix. Gently fold in the walnuts. Pour into the prepared loaf pan and spread to distribute evenly. Place the loaf pan in the air fryer basket and bake for 20 to 23 minutes, or until golden brown on top and a toothpick inserted into the center comes out clean. Allow to cool for 5 minutes before serving.

Cheddar-Ham-Corn Muffins

Prep time: 10 minutes | Cook time: 6 to 8 minutes per batch | Makes 8 muffins

180 ml cornmeal/polenta
60 ml flour
1½ teaspoons baking powder
¼ teaspoon salt
1 egg, beaten
2 tablespoons rapeseed oil
120 ml milk
120 ml shredded sharp Cheddar cheese
120 ml diced ham
8 foil muffin cups, liners removed and sprayed with cooking spray

Preheat the air fryer to 200°C. In a medium bowl, stir together the cornmeal, flour, baking powder, and salt. Add egg, oil, and milk to dry ingredients and mix well. Stir in shredded cheese and diced ham. Divide batter among the muffin cups. Place 4 filled muffin cups in air fryer basket and bake for 5 minutes. Reduce temperature to 166°C and bake for 1 to 2 minutes or until toothpick inserted in center of muffin comes out clean. Repeat steps 6 and 7 to cook remaining muffins.

Ham and Cheese Crescents

Prep time: 5 minutes | Cook time: 7 minutes | Makes 8 rolls

Oil, for spraying
1 (230 g) can ready-to-bake croissants
4 slices wafer-thin ham
8 cheese slices
2 tablespoons unsalted butter, melted

Line the air fryer basket with parchment and spray lightly with oil. Separate the dough into 8 pieces. Tear the ham slices in half and place 1 piece on each piece of dough. Top each with 1 slice of cheese. Roll up each piece of dough, starting on the wider side. Place the rolls in the prepared basket. Brush with the melted butter. Air fry at 160°C for 6 to 7 minutes, or until puffed and golden brown and the cheese is melted.

Classic British Breakfast

Prep time: 5 minutes | Cook time: 25 minutes | Serves 2

235 ml potatoes, sliced and diced
475 ml baked beans
2 eggs
1 tablespoon olive oil
1 sausage
Salt, to taste

Preheat the air fryer to 200°C and allow to warm. Break the eggs onto a baking dish and sprinkle with salt. Lay the beans on the dish, next to the eggs. In a bowl, coat the potatoes with the olive oil. Sprinkle with salt. Transfer the bowl of potato slices to the air fryer and bake for 10 minutes. Swap out the bowl of potatoes for the dish containing the eggs and beans. Bake for another 10 minutes. Cover the potatoes with parchment paper. Slice up the sausage and throw the slices on top of the beans and eggs. Bake for another 5 minutes. Serve with the potatoes.

Maple Granola

Prep time: 5 minutes | Cook time: 40 minutes | Makes 475 ml

235 ml rolled oats
3 tablespoons pure maple syrup
1 tablespoon sugar
1 tablespoon neutral-flavored oil, such as refined coconut or sunflower

¼ teaspoon sea salt
¼ teaspoon ground cinnamon
¼ teaspoon vanilla extract

Insert the crisper plate into the basket and the basket into the unit. Preheat the unit by selecting BAKE, setting the temperature to 120°C, and setting the time to 3 minutes. Select START/STOP to begin. In a medium bowl, stir together the oats, maple syrup, sugar, oil, salt, cinnamon, and vanilla until thoroughly combined. Transfer the granola to a 6-by-2-inch round baking pan. Once the unit is preheated, place the pan into the basket. Select BAKE, set the temperature to 120°C and set the time to 40 minutes. Select START/STOP to begin. After 10 minutes, stir the granola well. Resume cooking, stirring the granola every 10 minutes, for a total of 40 minutes, or until the granola is lightly browned and mostly dry. When the cooking is complete, place the granola on a plate to cool. It will become crisp as it cools. Store the completely cooled granola in an airtight container in a cool, dry place for 1 to 2 weeks.

Double-Dipped Mini Cinnamon Biscuits

Prep time: 15 minutes | Cook time: 13 minutes | Makes 8 biscuits

475 ml blanched almond flour
120 ml liquid or powdered sweetener
1 teaspoon baking powder
½ teaspoon fine sea salt
60 ml plus 2 tablespoons (¾ stick) very cold unsalted butter
60 ml unsweetened, unflavoured almond milk

1 large egg
1 teaspoon vanilla extract
3 teaspoons ground cinnamon
Glaze:
120 ml powdered sweetener
60 ml double cream or unsweetened, unflavoured almond milk

Preheat the air fryer to 176°C. Line a pie pan that fits into your air fryer with parchment paper. In a medium-sized bowl, mix together the almond flour, sweetener (if powdered; do not add liquid sweetener), baking powder, and salt. Cut the butter into ½-inch squares, then use a hand mixer to work the butter into the dry ingredients. When you are done, the mixture should still have chunks of butter. In a small bowl, whisk together the almond milk, egg, and vanilla extract (if using liquid sweetener, add it as well) until blended. Using a fork, stir the wet ingredients into the dry ingredients until large clumps form. Add the cinnamon and use your hands to swirl it into the dough. Form the dough into sixteen 1-inch balls and place them on the prepared pan, spacing them about ½ inch apart. (If you're using a smaller air fryer, work in batches if necessary.) Bake in the air fryer until golden, 10 to 13 minutes. Remove from the air fryer and let cool on the pan for at least 5 minutes. While the biscuits bake, make the glaze: Place the powdered sweetener in a small bowl and slowly stir in the heavy cream with a fork. When the biscuits have cooled somewhat, dip the tops into the glaze, allow it to dry a bit, and then dip again for a thick glaze. Serve warm or at room temperature. Store unglazed biscuits in an airtight container in the refrigerator for up to 3 days or in the freezer for up to a month. Reheat in a preheated 176°C air fryer for 5 minutes, or until warmed through, and dip in the glaze as instructed above.

Bacon, Egg, and Cheese Roll Ups

Prep time: 15 minutes | Cook time: 15 minutes | Serves 4

2 tablespoons unsalted butter
60 ml chopped onion
½ medium green pepper, seeded and chopped
6 large eggs

12 slices bacon
235 ml shredded sharp Cheddar cheese
120 ml mild salsa, for dipping

In a medium skillet over medium heat, melt butter. Add onion and pepper to the skillet and sauté until fragrant and onions are translucent, about 3 minutes. Whisk eggs in a small bowl and pour into skillet. Scramble eggs with onions and peppers until fluffy and fully cooked, about 5 minutes. Remove from heat and set aside. On work surface, place three slices of bacon side by side, overlapping about ¼ inch. Place 60 ml scrambled eggs in a heap on the side closest to you and sprinkle 60 ml cheese on top of the eggs. Tightly roll the bacon around the eggs and secure the seam with a toothpick if necessary. Place each roll into the air fryer basket. Adjust the temperature to 176°C and air fry for 15 minutes. Rotate the rolls halfway through the cooking time. Bacon will be brown and crispy when completely cooked. Serve immediately with salsa for dipping.

Honey-Apricot Granola with Greek Yoghurt

Prep time: 10 minutes | Cook time: 30 minutes | Serves 6

235 ml rolled oats
60 ml dried apricots, diced
60 ml almond slivers
60 ml walnuts, chopped
60 ml pumpkin seeds
60 to 80 ml honey, plus more for drizzling
1 tablespoon olive oil

1 teaspoon ground cinnamon
¼ teaspoon ground nutmeg
¼ teaspoon salt
2 tablespoons sugar-free dark chocolate chips (optional)
700 ml fat-free plain Greek yoghurt

Preheat the air fryer to 128°C. Line the air fryer basket with parchment paper. In a large bowl, combine the oats, apricots, almonds, walnuts, pumpkin seeds, honey, olive oil, cinnamon, nutmeg, and salt, mixing so that the honey, oil, and spices are well distributed. Pour the mixture onto the parchment paper and spread it into an even layer. Bake for 10 minutes, then shake or stir and spread back out into an even layer. Continue baking for 10 minutes more, then repeat the process of shaking or stirring the mixture. Bake for an additional 10 minutes before removing from the air fryer. Allow the granola to cool completely before stirring in the chocolate chips (if using) and pouring into an airtight container for storage. For each serving, top 120 ml Greek yoghurt with 80 ml granola and a drizzle of honey, if needed.

Oat Bran Muffins

Prep time: 10 minutes | Cook time: 10 to 12 minutes per batch | Makes 8 muffins

160 ml oat bran
120 ml flour
60 ml brown sugar
1 teaspoon baking powder
½ teaspoon baking soda
⅛ teaspoon salt
120 ml buttermilk

1 egg
2 tablespoons rapeseed oil
120 ml chopped dates, raisins, or dried cranberries
24 paper muffin cups
Cooking spray

Preheat the air fryer to 166°C. In a large bowl, combine the oat bran, flour, brown sugar, baking powder, baking soda, and salt. In a small bowl, beat together the buttermilk, egg, and oil. Pour buttermilk mixture into bowl with dry ingredients and stir just until moistened. Do not beat. Gently stir in dried fruit. Use triple baking cups to help muffins hold shape during baking. Spray them with cooking spray, place 4 sets of cups in air fryer basket at a time, and fill each one ¾ full of batter. Cook for 10 to 12 minutes, until top springs back when lightly touched and toothpick inserted in center comes out clean. Repeat for remaining muffins.

Cauliflower Avocado Toast

Prep time: 15 minutes | Cook time: 8 minutes | Serves 2

1 (40 g) steamer bag cauliflower
1 large egg
120 ml shredded Mozzarella cheese

1 ripe medium avocado
½ teaspoon garlic powder
¼ teaspoon ground black pepper

Cook cauliflower according to package instructions. Remove from bag and place into cheesecloth or clean towel to remove excess moisture. Place cauliflower into a large bowl and mix in egg and Mozzarella. Cut a piece of parchment to fit your air fryer basket. Separate the cauliflower mixture into two, and place it on the parchment in two mounds. Press out the cauliflower mounds into a ¼-inch-thick rectangle. Place the parchment into the air fryer basket. Adjust the temperature to 204°C and set the timer for 8 minutes. Flip the cauliflower halfway through the cooking time. When the timer beeps, remove the parchment and allow the cauliflower to cool 5 minutes. Cut open the avocado and remove the pit. Scoop out the inside, place it in a medium bowl, and mash it with garlic powder and pepper. Spread onto the cauliflower. Serve immediately.

Fried Chicken Wings with Waffles

Prep time: 10 minutes | Cook time: 30 minutes | Serves 4

8 whole chicken wings
1 teaspoon garlic powder
Chicken seasoning, for preparing the chicken
Freshly ground black pepper, to taste

120 ml plain flour
Cooking oil spray
8 frozen waffles
Pure maple syrup, for serving (optional)

In a medium bowl, combine the chicken and garlic powder and season with chicken seasoning and pepper. Toss to coat. Transfer the chicken to a resealable plastic bag and add the flour. Seal the bag and shake it to coat the chicken thoroughly. Insert the crisper plate into the basket and the basket into the unit. Preheat the unit by selecting AIR FRY, setting the temperature to 204°C, and setting the time to 3 minutes. Select START/STOP to begin. Once the unit is preheated, spray the crisper plate with cooking oil. Using tongs, transfer the chicken from the bag to the basket. It is okay to stack the chicken wings on top of each other. Spray them with cooking oil. Select AIR FRY, set the temperature to 204°C, and set the time to 20 minutes. Select START/STOP to begin. After 5 minutes, remove the basket and shake the wings. Reinsert the basket to resume cooking. Remove and shake the basket every 5 minutes until the chicken is fully cooked. When the cooking is complete, remove the cooked chicken from the basket; cover to keep warm. Rinse the basket and crisper plate with warm water. Insert them back into the unit. Select AIR FRY, set the temperature to 182°C, and set the time to 3 minutes. Select START/STOP to begin. 1Once the unit is preheated, spray the crisper plate with cooking spray. Working in batches, place the frozen waffles into the basket. Do not stack them. Spray the waffles with cooking oil. 1Select AIR FRY, set the temperature to 182°C, and set the time to 6 minutes. Select START/STOP to begin. 1When the cooking is complete, repeat steps 10 and 11 with the remaining waffles. 1Serve the waffles with the chicken and a touch of maple syrup, if desired.

Banana-Nut Muffins

Prep time: 5 minutes | Cook time: 15 minutes | Makes 10 muffins

Oil, for spraying
2 very ripe bananas
120 ml packed light brown sugar
80 ml rapeseed oil or vegetable oil

1 large egg
1 teaspoon vanilla extract
180 ml plain flour
1 teaspoon baking powder
1 teaspoon ground cinnamon
120 ml chopped walnuts

Preheat the air fryer to 160°C. Spray 10 silicone muffin cups lightly with oil. In a medium bowl, mash the bananas. Add the brown sugar, rapeseed oil, egg, and vanilla and stir to combine. Fold in the flour, baking powder, and cinnamon until just combined. Add the walnuts and fold a few times to distribute throughout the batter. Divide the batter equally among the prepared muffin cups and place them in the basket. You may need to work in batches, depending on the size of your air fryer. Cook for 15 minutes, or until golden brown and a toothpick inserted into the center of a muffin comes out clean. The air fryer tends to brown muffins more than the oven, so don't be alarmed if they are darker than you're used to. They will still taste great. Let cool on a wire rack before serving.

Chapter 4 Pizzas, Wraps, and Sandwiches

Chapter 4 Pizzas, Wraps, and Sandwiches

Crispy Chicken Egg Rolls

Prep time: 10 minutes | Cook time: 23 to 24 minutes | Serves 4

450 g minced chicken
2 teaspoons olive oil
2 garlic cloves, minced
1 teaspoon grated fresh ginger
475 ml white cabbage, shredded

1 onion, chopped
60 ml soy sauce
8 egg roll wrappers
1 egg, beaten
Cooking spray

Preheat the air fryer to 188°C. Spritz the air fryer basket with cooking spray. Heat olive oil in a saucepan over medium heat. Sauté the garlic and ginger in the olive oil for 1 minute, or until fragrant. Add the minced chicken to the saucepan. Sauté for 5 minutes, or until the chicken is cooked through. Add the cabbage, onion and soy sauce and sauté for 5 to 6 minutes, or until the vegetables become soft. Remove the saucepan from the heat. Unfold the egg roll wrappers on a clean work surface. Divide the chicken mixture among the wrappers and brush the edges of the wrappers with the beaten egg. Tightly roll up the egg rolls, enclosing the filling. Arrange the rolls in the prepared air fryer basket and air fry for 12 minutes, or until crispy and golden brown. Turn halfway through the cooking time to ensure even cooking. Transfer to a platter and let cool for 5 minutes before serving.

Spinach and Ricotta Pockets

Prep time: 20 minutes | Cook time: 10 minutes per batch | Makes 8 pockets

2 large eggs, divided
1 tablespoon water
235 ml baby spinach, roughly chopped
60 ml sun-dried tomatoes, finely chopped
235 ml ricotta cheese

235 ml basil, chopped
¼ teaspoon red pepper flakes
¼ teaspoon rock salt
2 refrigerated rolled sheets of shortcrust pastry
2 tablespoons sesame seeds

Preheat the air fryer to 192°C. Spritz the air fryer basket with cooking spray. Whisk an egg with water in a small bowl. Combine the spinach, tomatoes, the other egg, ricotta cheese, basil, red pepper flakes, and salt in a large bowl. Whisk to mix well. Unfold the pastry on a clean work surface and slice each sheet into 4 wedges. Scoop up 3 tablespoons of the spinach mixture on each wedge and leave ½ inch space from edges. Fold the wedges in half to wrap the filling and press the edges with a fork to seal. Arrange the wraps in the preheated air fryer and spritz with cooking spray. Sprinkle with sesame seeds. Work in 4 batches to avoid overcrowding. Air fry for 10 minutes or until crispy and golden. Flip them halfway through. Serve immediately.

Portobello Pizzas

Prep time: 10 minutes | Cook time: 10 minutes | Serves 4

Olive oil
4 large portobello mushroom caps, cleaned and stems removed
Garlic powder

8 tablespoons pizza sauce
16 slices turkey pepperoni
8 tablespoons Mozzarella cheese

Spray the air fryer basket lightly with olive oil. Lightly spray the outside of the mushrooms with olive oil and sprinkle with a little garlic powder, to taste. Turn the mushroom over and lightly spray the sides and top edges of the mushroom with olive oil and sprinkle with garlic powder, to taste. Place the mushrooms in the air fryer basket in a single layer with the top side down. Leave room between the mushrooms. You may need to cook them in batches. Air fry at 176°C for 5 minutes. Spoon 2 tablespoons of pizza sauce on each mushroom. Top each with 4 slices of turkey pepperoni and sprinkle with 2 tablespoons of Mozzarella cheese. Press the pepperoni and cheese down into the pizza sauce to help prevent it from flying around inside the air fryer. Air fry until the cheese is melted and lightly browned on top, another 3 to 5 minutes.

Cheesy Veggie Wraps

Prep time: 15 minutes | Cook time: 8 to 10 minutes per batch | Serves 4

227 g green beans
2 portobello mushroom caps, sliced
1 large red pepper, sliced
2 tablespoons olive oil, divided
¼ teaspoon salt
1 (425 g) can chickpeas, drained

3 tablespoons lemon juice
¼ teaspoon ground black pepper
4 (6-inch) wholemeal wraps
110 g fresh herb or garlic goat cheese, crumbled
1 lemon, cut into wedges

Preheat the air fryer to 204°C. Add the green beans, mushrooms, red pepper to a large bowl. Drizzle with 1 tablespoon olive oil and season with salt. Toss until well coated. Transfer the vegetable mixture to a baking pan. Air fry in the preheated air fryer in 2 batches, 8 to 10 minutes per batch, stirring constantly during cooking. Meanwhile, mash the chickpeas with lemon juice, pepper and the remaining 1 tablespoon oil until well blended Unfold the wraps on a clean work surface. Spoon the chickpea mash on the wraps and spread all over. Divide the cooked veggies among wraps. Sprinkle 30 g crumbled goat cheese on top of each wrap. Fold to wrap. Squeeze the lemon wedges on top and serve.

English Muffin Tuna Sandwiches

Prep time: 8 minutes | Cook time: 5 minutes | Serves 4

1 (170 g) can chunk light tuna, drained
60 ml mayonnaise
2 tablespoons mustard
1 tablespoon lemon juice
2 spring onions, minced

3 English muffins, split with a fork
3 tablespoons softened butter
6 thin slices provolone or Muenster cheese

In a small bowl, combine the tuna, mayonnaise, mustard, lemon juice, and spring onions. Butter the cut side of the English muffins. Air fry butter-side up in the air fryer at 200ºC for 2 to 4 minutes or until light golden brown. Remove the muffins from the air fryer basket. Top each muffin with one slice of cheese and return to the air fryer. Air fry for 2 to 4 minutes or until the cheese melts and starts to brown. Remove the muffins from the air fryer, top with the tuna mixture, and serve.

Korean Flavour Beef and Onion Tacos

Prep time: 1 hour 15 minutes | Cook time: 12 minutes | Serves 6

2 tablespoons gochujang chilli sauce
1 tablespoon soy sauce
2 tablespoons sesame seeds
2 teaspoons minced fresh ginger
2 cloves garlic, minced
2 tablespoons toasted sesame oil
2 teaspoons sugar

½ teaspoon rock salt
680 g thinly sliced braising steak
1 medium red onion, sliced
6 corn tortillas, warmed
60 ml chopped fresh coriander
120 ml kimchi
120 ml chopped spring onions

Combine the gochujang, soy sauce, sesame seeds, ginger, garlic, sesame oil, sugar, and salt in a large bowl. Stir to mix well. Dunk the braising steak in the large bowl. Press to submerge, then wrap the bowl in plastic and refrigerate to marinate for at least 1 hour. Preheat the air fryer to 204ºC. Remove the braising steak from the marinade and transfer to the preheated air fryer basket. Add the onion and air fry for 12 minutes or until well browned. Shake the basket halfway through. Unfold the tortillas on a clean work surface, then divide the fried beef and onion on the tortillas. Spread the coriander, kimchi, and spring onions on top. Serve immediately.

Barbecue Chicken Pitta Pizza

Prep time: 5 minutes | Cook time: 5 to 7 minutes per batch | Makes 4 pizzas

235 ml barbecue sauce, divided
4 pitta breads
475 ml shredded cooked chicken
475 ml shredded Mozzarella

cheese
½ small red onion, thinly sliced
2 tablespoons finely chopped fresh coriander

Measure 120 ml of the barbecue sauce in a small measuring cup. Spread 2 tablespoons of the barbecue sauce on each pitta. In a medium bowl, mix together the remaining 120 ml of barbecue sauce and chicken. Place 120 ml of the chicken on each pitta. Top each pizza with 120 ml of the Mozzarella cheese. Sprinkle the tops of the pizzas with the red onion. Place one pizza in the air fryer. Air fry at 204ºC for 5 to 7 minutes. Repeat this process with the remaining pizzas. Top the pizzas with the coriander.

Bacon and Pepper Sandwiches

Prep time: 15 minutes | Cook time: 7 minutes | Serves 4

80 ml spicy barbecue sauce
2 tablespoons honey
8 slices precooked bacon, cut into thirds
1 red pepper, sliced

1 yellow pepper, sliced
3 pitta pockets, cut in half
300 ml torn butterhead lettuce leaves
2 tomatoes, sliced

In a small bowl, combine the barbecue sauce and the honey. Brush this mixture lightly onto the bacon slices and the red and yellow pepper slices. Put the peppers into the air fryer basket and air fry at 176ºC for 4 minutes. Then shake the basket, add the bacon, and air fry for 2 minutes or until the bacon is browned and the peppers are tender. Fill the pitta halves with the bacon, peppers, any remaining barbecue sauce, lettuce, and tomatoes, and serve immediately.

Mexican Flavour Chicken Burgers

Prep time: 15 minutes | Cook time: 20 minutes | Serves 6 to 8

4 skinless and boneless chicken breasts
1 small head of cauliflower, sliced into florets
1 jalapeño pepper
3 tablespoons smoked paprika
1 tablespoon thyme
1 tablespoon oregano
1 tablespoon mustard powder
1 teaspoon cayenne pepper

1 egg
Salt and ground black pepper, to taste
2 tomatoes, sliced
2 lettuce leaves, chopped
6 to 8 brioche buns, sliced lengthwise
180 ml taco sauce
Cooking spray

Preheat the air fryer to 176ºC and spritz with cooking spray. In a blender, add the cauliflower florets, jalapeño pepper, paprika, thyme, oregano, mustard powder and cayenne pepper and blend until the mixture has a texture similar to breadcrumbs. Transfer ¾ of the cauliflower mixture to a medium bowl and set aside. Beat the egg in a different bowl and set aside. Add the chicken breasts to the blender with remaining cauliflower mixture. Sprinkle with salt and pepper. Blend until finely chopped and well mixed. Remove the mixture from the blender and form into 6 to 8 patties. One by one, dredge each patty in the reserved cauliflower mixture, then into the egg. Dip them in the cauliflower mixture again for additional coating. Place the coated patties into the air fryer basket and spritz with cooking spray. Air fry for 20 minutes or until golden and crispy. Flip halfway through to ensure even cooking. Transfer the patties to a clean work surface and assemble with the buns, tomato slices, chopped lettuce leaves and taco sauce to make burgers. Serve and enjoy.

Jerk Chicken Wraps

Prep time: 30 minutes | Cook time: 15 minutes | Serves 4

450 g boneless, skinless chicken tenderloins	235 ml julienned carrots
235 ml jerk marinade	235 ml peeled cucumber ribbons
Olive oil	235 ml shredded lettuce
4 large low-carb tortillas	235 ml mango or pineapple chunks

In a medium bowl, coat the chicken with the jerk marinade, cover, and refrigerate for 1 hour. Spray the air fryer basket lightly with olive oil. Place the chicken in the air fryer basket in a single layer and spray lightly with olive oil. You may need to cook the chicken in batches. Reserve any leftover marinade. Air fry at 192°C for 8 minutes. Turn the chicken over and brush with some of the remaining marinade. Cook until the chicken reaches an internal temperature of at least 74°C, an additional 5 to 7 minutes. To assemble the wraps, fill each tortilla with 60 ml carrots, 60 ml cucumber, 60 ml lettuce, and 60 ml mango. Place one quarter of the chicken tenderloins on top and roll up the tortilla. These are great served warm or cold.

Grilled Cheese Sandwich

Prep time: 5 minutes | Cook time: 5 minutes | Makes 2 sandwiches

4 slices bread	2 teaspoons butter or oil
110 g Cheddar cheese slices	

Lay the four cheese slices on two of the bread slices and top with the remaining two slices of bread. Brush both sides with butter or oil and cut the sandwiches in rectangular halves. Place in air fryer basket and air fry at 200°C for 5 minutes until the outside is crisp and the cheese melts.

Bacon Garlic Pizza

Prep time: 10 minutes | Cook time: 20 minutes | Serves 4

Flour, for dusting	½ teaspoon dried oregano
Non-stick baking spray with flour	½ teaspoon garlic salt
4 frozen large wholemeal bread rolls, thawed	8 slices precooked bacon, cut into 1-inch pieces
5 cloves garlic, minced	300 ml shredded Cheddar cheese
180 ml pizza sauce	

On a lightly floured surface, press out each bread roll to a 5-by-3-inch oval. Spray four 6-by-4-inch pieces of heavy-duty foil with non-stick spray and place one crust on each piece. Bake, two at a time, at 188°C for 2 minutes or until the crusts are set, but not browned. Meanwhile, in a small bowl, combine the garlic, pizza sauce, oregano, and garlic salt. When the pizza crusts are set, spread each with some of the sauce. Top with the bacon pieces and Cheddar cheese. Bake, two at a time, for another 8 minutes or until the crust is browned and the cheese is melted and starting to brown.

Beans and Greens Pizza

Prep time: 11 minutes | Cook time: 14 to 19 minutes | Serves 4

180 ml wholemeal pastry flour	235 ml canned no-added-salt cannellini beans, rinsed and drained
½ teaspoon low-salt baking powder	
1 tablespoon olive oil, divided	½ teaspoon dried thyme
235 ml chopped kale	1 piece low-salt string cheese, torn into pieces
475 ml chopped fresh baby spinach	

In a small bowl, mix the pastry flour and baking powder until well combined. Add 60 ml water and 2 teaspoons of olive oil. Mix until a dough forms. On a floured surface, press or roll the dough into a 7-inch round. Set aside while you cook the greens. In a baking pan, mix the kale, spinach, and remaining teaspoon of the olive oil. Air fry at 176°C for 3 to 5 minutes, until the greens are wilted. Drain well. Put the pizza dough into the air fryer basket. Top with the greens, cannellini beans, thyme, and string cheese. Air fry for 11 to 14 minutes, or until the crust is golden brown and the cheese is melted. Cut into quarters to serve.

Mediterranean-Pitta Wraps

Prep time: 5 minutes | Cook time: 14 minutes | Serves 4

450 g mackerel fish fillets	Sea salt and freshly ground black pepper, to taste
2 tablespoons olive oil	
1 tablespoon Mediterranean seasoning mix	60 g feta cheese, crumbled
½ teaspoon chilli powder	4 tortillas

Toss the fish fillets with the olive oil; place them in the lightly oiled air fryer basket. Air fry the fish fillets at 204°C for about 14 minutes, turning them over halfway through the cooking time. Assemble your pittas with the chopped fish and remaining ingredients and serve warm.

Nugget and Veggie Taco Wraps

Prep time: 5 minutes | Cook time: 15 minutes | Serves 4

1 tablespoon water	1 small red pepper, chopped
4 pieces commercial vegan nuggets, chopped	2 cobs grilled corn kernels
1 small brown onion, diced	4 large corn tortillas
	Mixed greens, for garnish

Preheat the air fryer to 204°C. Over a medium heat, sauté the nuggets in the water with the onion, corn kernels and pepper in a skillet, then remove from the heat. Fill the tortillas with the nuggets and vegetables and fold them up. Transfer to the inside of the fryer and air fry for 15 minutes. Once crispy, serve immediately, garnished with the mixed greens.

Air Fried Philly Cheesesteaks

Prep time: 20 minutes | Cook time: 20 minutes | Serves 2

340 g boneless rib-eye steak, sliced thinly
½ teaspoon Worcestershire sauce
½ teaspoon soy sauce
Rock salt and ground black pepper, to taste
½ green pepper, stemmed, deseeded, and thinly sliced
½ small onion, halved and thinly sliced
1 tablespoon vegetable oil
2 soft sub rolls, split three-fourths of the way through
1 tablespoon butter, softened
2 slices provolone cheese, halved

Preheat the air fryer to 204°C. Combine the steak, Worcestershire sauce, soy sauce, salt, and ground black pepper in a large bowl. Toss to coat well. Set aside. Combine the pepper, onion, salt, ground black pepper, and vegetable oil in a separate bowl. Toss to coat the vegetables well. Pour the steak and vegetables in the preheated air fryer. Air fry for 15 minutes or until the steak is browned and vegetables are tender. Transfer them on a plate. Set aside. Brush the sub rolls with butter, then place in the air fryer to toast for 3 minutes or until lightly browned. Transfer the rolls on a clean work surface and divide the steak and vegetable mix in between the rolls. Spread with cheese. Arrange the rolls in the air fryer and air fry for 2 minutes or until the cheese melts. Serve immediately.

Barbecue Pulled Pork Sandwiches

Prep time: 15 minutes | Cook time: 30 minutes | Serves 4

350 ml prepared barbecue sauce
2 tablespoons distilled white vinegar
2 tablespoons light brown sugar
1 tablespoon minced garlic
1 teaspoon hot sauce
900 g pork shoulder roast
1 to 2 tablespoons oil
4 sandwich buns

In a medium bowl, stir together the barbecue sauce, vinegar, brown sugar, garlic, and hot sauce. Preheat the air fryer to 182°C. Line the air fryer basket with parchment paper and spritz it with oil. Place the pork on the parchment and baste it with a thick layer of sauce. Cook for 5 minutes. Flip the pork and baste with sauce. Repeat 3 more times for a total of 20 minutes of cook time, ending with basting. Increase the air fryer temperature to 200°C. Cook the pork for 5 minutes. Flip and baste. Cook for 5 minutes more. Flip and baste. Let sit for 5 minutes before pulling the pork into 1-inch pieces. Transfer to a bowl and toss the pork with the remaining sauce. Serve on buns.

Pesto Chicken Mini Pizzas

Prep time: 5 minutes | Cook time: 10 minutes | Serves 4
475 ml shredded cooked chicken
180 ml pesto
4 English muffins, split
475 ml shredded Mozzarella cheese

In a medium bowl, toss the chicken with the pesto. Place one-eighth of the chicken on each English muffin half. Top each English muffin with 60 ml Mozzarella cheese. Put four pizzas at a time in the air fryer and air fry at 176°C for 5 minutes. Repeat this process with the other four pizzas.

Tuna Wraps

Prep time: 10 minutes | Cook time: 4 to 7 minutes | Serves 4

450 g fresh tuna steak, cut into 1-inch cubes
1 tablespoon grated fresh ginger
2 garlic cloves, minced
½ teaspoon toasted sesame oil
4 low-salt wholemeal tortillas
60 ml low-fat mayonnaise
475 ml shredded romaine lettuce
1 red pepper, thinly sliced

In a medium bowl, mix the tuna, ginger, garlic, and sesame oil. Let it stand for 10 minutes. Air fry the tuna in the air fryer at 200°C for 4 to 7 minutes, or until done to your liking and lightly browned. Make wraps with the tuna, tortillas, mayonnaise, lettuce, and pepper. Serve immediately.

Beef and Pepper Fajitas

Prep time: 15 minutes | Cook time: 10 minutes | Serves 4

450 g beef sirloin steak, cut into strips
2 shallots, sliced
1 orange pepper, sliced
1 red pepper, sliced
2 garlic cloves, minced
2 tablespoons Cajun seasoning
1 tablespoon paprika
Salt and ground black pepper, to taste
4 corn tortillas
120 ml shredded Cheddar cheese
Cooking spray

Preheat the air fryer to 182°C and spritz with cooking spray. Combine all the ingredients, except for the tortillas and cheese, in a large bowl. Toss to coat well. Pour the beef and vegetables in the preheated air fryer and spritz with cooking spray. Air fry for 10 minutes or until the meat is browned and the vegetables are soft and lightly wilted. Shake the basket halfway through. Unfold the tortillas on a clean work surface and spread the cooked beef and vegetables on top. Scatter with cheese and fold to serve.

Chapter 5 Vegetables and Sides

Baked Jalapeño and Cheese Cauliflower Mash

Prep time: 10 minutes | Cook time: 15 minutes | Serves 6

1 (340 g) steamer bag cauliflower florets, cooked according to package instructions
2 tablespoons salted butter, softened

60 g cream cheese, softened
120 g shredded sharp Cheddar cheese
20 g pickled jalapeños
½ teaspoon salt
¼ teaspoon ground black pepper

Place cooked cauliflower into a food processor with remaining ingredients. Pulse twenty times until cauliflower is smooth and all ingredients are combined. Spoon mash into an ungreased round nonstick baking dish. Place dish into air fryer basket. Adjust the temperature to 192ºC and bake for 15 minutes. The top will be golden brown when done. Serve warm.

Spinach and Sweet Pepper Poppers

Prep time: 10 minutes | Cook time: 8 minutes | Makes 16 poppers

110 g cream cheese, softened
20 g chopped fresh spinach leaves
½ teaspoon garlic powder

8 mini sweet bell peppers, tops removed, seeded, and halved lengthwise

In a medium bowl, mix cream cheese, spinach, and garlic powder. Place 1 tablespoon mixture into each sweet pepper half and press down to smooth. Place poppers into ungreased air fryer basket. Adjust the temperature to 200ºC and air fry for 8 minutes. Poppers will be done when cheese is browned on top and peppers are tender-crisp. Serve warm.

Curried Fruit

Prep time: 10 minutes | Cook time: 20 minutes | Serves 6 to 8

210 g cubed fresh pineapple
200 g cubed fresh pear (firm, not overly ripe)
230 g frozen peaches, thawed

425 g can dark, sweet, pitted cherries with juice
2 tablespoons brown sugar
1 teaspoon curry powder

Combine all ingredients in large bowl. Stir gently to mix in the sugar and curry. Pour into a baking pan and bake at 180ºC for 10 minutes. Stir fruit and cook 10 more minutes. Serve hot.

Courgette Balls

Prep time: 5 minutes | Cook time: 10 minutes | Serves 4

4 courgettes
1 egg
45 g grated Parmesan cheese

1 tablespoon Italian herbs
75 g grated coconut

Thinly grate the courgettes and dry with a cheesecloth, ensuring to remove all the moisture. In a bowl, combine the courgettes with the egg, Parmesan, Italian herbs, and grated coconut, mixing well to incorporate everything. Using the hands, mold the mixture into balls. Preheat the air fryer to 200ºC. Lay the courgette balls in the air fryer basket and air fry for 10 minutes. Serve hot.

Blistered Shishito Peppers with Lime Juice

Prep time: 5 minutes | Cook time: 9 minutes | Serves 3

230 g shishito peppers, rinsed
Cooking spray
Sauce:

1 tablespoon tamari or shoyu
2 teaspoons fresh lime juice
2 large garlic cloves, minced

Preheat the air fryer to 200ºC. Spritz the air fryer basket with cooking spray. Place the shishito peppers in the basket and spritz them with cooking spray. Roast for 3 minutes. Meanwhile, whisk together all the ingredients for the sauce in a large bowl. Set aside. Shake the basket and spritz them with cooking spray again, then roast for an additional 3 minutes. Shake the basket one more time and spray the peppers with cooking spray. Continue roasting for 3 minutes until the peppers are blistered and nicely browned. Remove the peppers from the basket to the bowl of sauce. Toss to coat well and serve immediately.

Tingly Chili-Roasted Broccoli

Prep time: 5 minutes | Cook time: 10 minutes | Serves 2

340 g broccoli florets
2 tablespoons Asian hot chili oil
1 teaspoon ground Sichuan peppercorns (or black pepper)
2 garlic cloves, finely chopped

1 (2-inch) piece fresh ginger, peeled and finely chopped
coarse sea salt and freshly ground black pepper, to taste

In a bowl, toss together the broccoli, chili oil, Sichuan peppercorns, garlic, ginger, and salt and black pepper to taste. Transfer to the air fryer and roast at 192ºC, shaking the basket halfway through, until lightly charred and tender, about 10 minutes. Remove from the air fryer and serve warm.

Roasted Radishes with Sea Salt

Prep time: 5 minutes | Cook time: 18 minutes | Serves 4

450 g radishes, ends trimmed if needed

2 tablespoons olive oil
½ teaspoon sea salt

Preheat the air fryer to 180ºC. In a large bowl, combine the radishes with olive oil and sea salt. Pour the radishes into the air fryer and roast for 10 minutes. Stir or turn the radishes over and roast for 8 minutes more, then serve.

Cauliflower with Lime Juice

Prep time: 10 minutes | Cook time: 7 minutes | Serves 4

215 g chopped cauliflower florets
2 tablespoons coconut oil, melted

2 teaspoons chili powder
½ teaspoon garlic powder
1 medium lime
2 tablespoons chopped coriander

In a large bowl, toss cauliflower with coconut oil. Sprinkle with chili powder and garlic powder. Place seasoned cauliflower into the air fryer basket. Adjust the temperature to 180ºC and set the timer for 7 minutes. Cauliflower will be tender and begin to turn golden at the edges. Place into a serving bowl. Cut the lime into quarters and squeeze juice over cauliflower. Garnish with coriander.

Garlic Courgette and Red Peppers

Prep time: 5 minutes | Cook time: 15 minutes | Serves 6

2 medium courgette, cubed
1 red pepper, diced
2 garlic cloves, sliced

2 tablespoons olive oil
½ teaspoon salt

Preheat the air fryer to 193ºC. In a large bowl, mix together the courgette, bell pepper, and garlic with the olive oil and salt. Pour the mixture into the air fryer basket, and roast for 7 minutes. Shake or stir, then roast for 7 to 8 minutes more.

Dill-and-Garlic Beetroots

Prep time: 10 minutes | Cook time: 30 minutes | Serves 4

4 beetroots, cleaned, peeled, and sliced
1 garlic clove, minced
2 tablespoons chopped fresh dill

¼ teaspoon salt
¼ teaspoon black pepper
3 tablespoons olive oil

Preheat the air fryer to 192ºC. In a large bowl, mix together all of the ingredients so the beetroots are well coated with the oil. Pour the beetroot mixture into the air fryer basket, and roast for 15 minutes before stirring, then continue roasting for 15 minutes more.

Garlic Cauliflower with Tahini

Prep time: 10 minutes | Cook time: 20 minutes | Serves 4

Cauliflower:
500 g cauliflower florets (about 1 large head)
6 garlic cloves, smashed and cut into thirds
3 tablespoons vegetable oil
½ teaspoon ground cumin
½ teaspoon ground coriander

½ teaspoon coarse sea salt
Sauce:
2 tablespoons tahini (sesame paste)
2 tablespoons hot water
1 tablespoon fresh lemon juice
1 teaspoon minced garlic
½ teaspoon coarse sea salt

For the cauliflower: In a large bowl, combine the cauliflower florets and garlic. Drizzle with the vegetable oil. Sprinkle with the cumin, coriander, and salt. Toss until well coated. Place the cauliflower in the air fryer basket. Set the air fryer to 200ºC for 20 minutes, turning the cauliflower halfway through the cooking time. Meanwhile, for the sauce: In a small bowl, combine the tahini, water, lemon juice, garlic, and salt. (The sauce will appear curdled at first, but keep stirring until you have a thick, creamy, smooth mixture.) Transfer the cauliflower to a large serving bowl. Pour the sauce over and toss gently to coat. Serve immediately.

Sweet and Crispy Roasted Pearl Onions

Prep time: 5 minutes | Cook time: 18 minutes | Serves 3

1 (410 g) package frozen pearl onions (do not thaw)
2 tablespoons extra-virgin olive oil
2 tablespoons balsamic vinegar

2 teaspoons finely chopped fresh rosemary
½ teaspoon coarse sea salt
¼ teaspoon black pepper

In a medium bowl, combine the onions, olive oil, vinegar, rosemary, salt, and pepper until well coated. Transfer the onions to the air fryer basket. Set the air fryer to 200ºC for 18 minutes, or until the onions are tender and lightly charred, stirring once or twice during the cooking time.

Bacon Potatoes and Green Beans

Prep time: 10 minutes | Cook time: 25 minutes | Serves 4

Oil, for spraying
900 g medium Maris Piper potatoes, quartered
100 g bacon bits

280 g fresh green beans
1 teaspoon salt
½ teaspoon freshly ground black pepper

Line the air fryer basket with parchment and spray lightly with oil. Place the potatoes in the prepared basket. Top with the bacon bits and green beans. Sprinkle with the salt and black pepper and spray liberally with oil. Air fry at 180ºC for 25 minutes, stirring after 12 minutes and spraying with oil, until the potatoes are easily pierced with a fork.

Gold Artichoke Hearts

Prep time: 15 minutes | Cook time: 8 minutes | Serves 4

12 whole artichoke hearts packed in water, drained
60 g plain flour
1 egg

40 g panko bread crumbs
1 teaspoon Italian seasoning
Cooking oil spray

Squeeze any excess water from the artichoke hearts and place them on paper towels to dry. Place the flour in a small bowl. In another small bowl, beat the egg. In a third small bowl, stir together the panko and Italian seasoning. Dip the artichoke hearts in the flour, in the egg, and into the panko mixture until coated. Insert the crisper plate into the basket and the basket into the unit. Preheat the unit by selecting AIR FRY, setting the temperature to 192ºC, and setting the time to 3 minutes. Select START/STOP to begin. Once the unit is preheated, spray the crisper plate and the basket with cooking oil. Place the breaded artichoke hearts into the basket, stacking them if needed. Select AIR FRY, set the temperature to 192ºC, and set the time to 8 minutes. Select START/STOP to begin. After 4 minutes, use tongs to flip the artichoke hearts. I recommend flipping instead of shaking because the hearts are small, and this will help keep the breading intact. Re-insert the basket to resume cooking. 1When the cooking is complete, the artichoke hearts should be deep golden brown and crisp. Cool for 5 minutes before serving.

Asparagus Fries

Prep time: 15 minutes | Cook time: 5 to 7 minutes per batch | Serves 4

340 g fresh asparagus spears with tough ends trimmed off
2 egg whites
60 ml water
80 g panko bread crumbs

25 g grated Parmesan cheese, plus 2 tablespoons
¼ teaspoon salt
Oil for misting or cooking spray

Preheat the air fryer to 200ºC. In a shallow dish, beat egg whites and water until slightly foamy. In another shallow dish, combine panko, Parmesan, and salt. Dip asparagus spears in egg, then roll in crumbs. Spray with oil or cooking spray. Place a layer of asparagus in air fryer basket, leaving just a little space in between each spear. Stack another layer on top, crosswise. Air fry at 200ºC for 5 to 7 minutes, until crispy and golden brown. Repeat to cook remaining asparagus.

Flatbread

Prep time: 5 minutes | Cook time: 7 minutes | Serves 2

225 g shredded Mozzarella cheese
25 g blanched finely ground

almond flour
30 g full-fat cream cheese, softened

In a large microwave-safe bowl, melt Mozzarella in the microwave for 30 seconds. Stir in almond flour until smooth and then add cream cheese. Continue mixing until dough forms, gently kneading

it with wet hands if necessary. Divide the dough into two pieces and roll out to ¼-inch thickness between two pieces of parchment. Cut another piece of parchment to fit your air fryer basket. Place a piece of flatbread onto your parchment and into the air fryer, working in two batches if needed. Adjust the temperature to 160ºC and air fry for 7 minutes. Halfway through the cooking time flip the flatbread. Serve warm.

Dijon Roast Cabbage

Prep time: 10 minutes | Cook time: 10 minutes | Serves 4

1 small head cabbage, cored and sliced into 1-inch-thick slices
2 tablespoons olive oil, divided
½ teaspoon salt

1 tablespoon Dijon mustard
1 teaspoon apple cider vinegar
1 teaspoon granular erythritol

Drizzle each cabbage slice with 1 tablespoon olive oil, then sprinkle with salt. Place slices into ungreased air fryer basket, working in batches if needed. Adjust the temperature to 180ºC and air fry for 10 minutes. Cabbage will be tender and edges will begin to brown when done. In a small bowl, whisk remaining olive oil with mustard, vinegar, and erythritol. Drizzle over cabbage in a large serving dish. Serve warm.

Creamed Asparagus

Prep time: 10 minutes | Cook time: 18 minutes | Serves 4

120 g whipping cream
45 g grated Parmesan cheese
60 g cream cheese, softened
450 g asparagus, ends trimmed,

chopped into 1-inch pieces
¼ teaspoon salt
¼ teaspoon ground black pepper

In a medium bowl, whisk together whipping cream, Parmesan, and cream cheese until combined. Place asparagus into an ungreased round nonstick baking dish. Pour cheese mixture over top and sprinkle with salt and pepper. Place dish into air fryer basket. Adjust the temperature to 180ºC and set the timer for 18 minutes. Asparagus will be tender when done. Serve warm.

Roasted Brussels Sprouts with Bacon

Prep time: 10 minutes | Cook time: 20 minutes | Serves 4

4 slices thick-cut bacon, chopped (about 110 g)
450 g Brussels sprouts, halved

(or quartered if large)
Freshly ground black pepper, to taste

Preheat the air fryer to 192ºC. Air fry the bacon for 5 minutes, shaking the basket once or twice during the cooking time. Add the Brussels sprouts to the basket and drizzle a little bacon fat from the bottom of the air fryer drawer into the basket. Toss the sprouts to coat with the bacon fat. Air fry for an additional 15 minutes, or until the Brussels sprouts are tender to a knifepoint. Season with freshly ground black pepper.

Broccoli-Cheddar Twice-Baked Potatoes

Prep time: 10 minutes | Cook time: 46 minutes | Serves 4

Oil, for spraying	1 tablespoon sour cream
2 medium Maris Piper potatoes	1 teaspoon garlic powder
1 tablespoon olive oil	1 teaspoon onion powder
30 g broccoli florets	60 g shredded Cheddar cheese

Line the air fryer basket with parchment and spray lightly with oil. Rinse the potatoes and pat dry with paper towels. Rub the outside of the potatoes with the olive oil and place them in the prepared basket. Air fry at 200ºC for 40 minutes, or until easily pierced with a fork. Let cool just enough to handle, then cut the potatoes in half lengthwise. Meanwhile, place the broccoli in a microwave-safe bowl, cover with water, and microwave on high for 5 to 8 minutes. Drain and set aside. Scoop out most of the potato flesh and transfer to a medium bowl. Add the sour cream, garlic, and onion powder and stir until the potatoes are mashed. Spoon the potato mixture back into the hollowed potato skins, mounding it to fit, if necessary. Top with the broccoli and cheese. Return the potatoes to the basket. You may need to work in batches, depending on the size of your air fryer. Air fry at 200ºC for 3 to 6 minutes, or until the cheese has melted. Serve immediately.

Air Fried Potatoes with Olives

Prep time: 15 minutes | Cook time: 40 minutes | Serves 1

1 medium Maris Piper potatoes, scrubbed and peeled	Dollop of butter
1 teaspoon olive oil	Dollop of cream cheese
¼ teaspoon onion powder	1 tablespoon Kalamata olives
⅛ teaspoon salt	1 tablespoon chopped chives

Preheat the air fryer to 200ºC. In a bowl, coat the potatoes with the onion powder, salt, olive oil, and butter. Transfer to the air fryer and air fry for 40 minutes, turning the potatoes over at the halfway point. Take care when removing the potatoes from the air fryer and serve with the cream cheese, Kalamata olives and chives on top.

"Faux-Tato" Hash

Prep time: 10 minutes | Cook time: 12 minutes | Serves 4

450 g radishes, ends removed, quartered	and chopped
¼ medium yellow onion, peeled and diced	2 tablespoons salted butter, melted
½ medium green pepper, seeded	½ teaspoon garlic powder
	¼ teaspoon ground black pepper

In a large bowl, combine radishes, onion, and bell pepper. Toss with butter. Sprinkle garlic powder and black pepper over mixture in bowl, then spoon into ungreased air fryer basket. Adjust the temperature to 160ºC and air fry for 12 minutes. Shake basket halfway through cooking. Radishes will be tender when done. Serve warm.

Crispy Garlic Sliced Aubergine

Prep time: 5 minutes | Cook time: 25 minutes | Serves 4

1 egg	½ teaspoon salt
1 tablespoon water	½ teaspoon paprika
60 g whole wheat bread crumbs	1 medium aubergine, sliced into
1 teaspoon garlic powder	¼-inch-thick rounds
½ teaspoon dried oregano	1 tablespoon olive oil

Preheat the air fryer to 180ºC. In a medium shallow bowl, beat together the egg and water until frothy. In a separate medium shallow bowl, mix together bread crumbs, garlic powder, oregano, salt, and paprika. Dip each aubergine slice into the egg mixture, then into the bread crumb mixture, coating the outside with crumbs. Place the slices in a single layer in the bottom of the air fryer basket. Drizzle the tops of the aubergine slices with the olive oil, then fry for 15 minutes. Turn each slice and cook for an additional 10 minutes.

Five-Spice Roasted Sweet Potatoes

Prep time: 10 minutes | Cook time: 12 minutes | Serves 4

½ teaspoon ground cinnamon	Freshly ground black pepper, to
¼ teaspoon ground cumin	taste
¼ teaspoon paprika	2 large sweet potatoes, peeled
1 teaspoon chili powder	and cut into ¾-inch cubes
⅛ teaspoon turmeric	1 tablespoon olive oil
½ teaspoon salt (optional)	

In a large bowl, mix together cinnamon, cumin, paprika, chili powder, turmeric, salt, and pepper to taste. Add potatoes and stir well. Drizzle the seasoned potatoes with the olive oil and stir until evenly coated. Place seasoned potatoes in a baking pan or an ovenproof dish that fits inside your air fryer basket. Cook for 6 minutes at 200ºC, stop, and stir well. Cook for an additional 6 minutes.

Curry Roasted Cauliflower

Prep time: 10 minutes | Cook time: 20 minutes | Serves 4

65 ml olive oil	1 head cauliflower, cut into bite-
2 teaspoons curry powder	size florets
½ teaspoon salt	½ red onion, sliced
¼ teaspoon freshly ground black pepper	2 tablespoons freshly chopped parsley, for garnish (optional)

Preheat the air fryer to 200ºC. In a large bowl, combine the olive oil, curry powder, salt, and pepper. Add the cauliflower and onion. Toss gently until the vegetables are completely coated with the oil mixture. Transfer the vegetables to the basket of the air fryer. Pausing about halfway through the cooking time to shake the basket, air fry for 20 minutes until the cauliflower is tender and beginning to brown. Top with the parsley, if desired, before serving.

Mole-Braised Cauliflower

Prep time: 10 minutes | Cook time: 15 minutes | Serves 2

230 g medium cauliflower florets
1 tablespoon vegetable oil
coarse sea salt and freshly ground black pepper, to taste
350 ml vegetable stock
2 tablespoons New Mexico chili powder (or regular chili powder)
2 tablespoons salted roasted

peanuts
1 tablespoon toasted sesame seeds, plus more for garnish
1 tablespoon finely chopped golden raisins
1 teaspoon coarse sea salt
1 teaspoon dark brown sugar
½ teaspoon dried oregano
¼ teaspoon cayenne pepper
⅛ teaspoon ground cinnamon

In a large bowl, toss the cauliflower with the oil and season with salt and black pepper. Transfer to a cake pan. Place the pan in the air fryer and roast at 192ºC until the cauliflower is tender and lightly browned at the edges, about 10 minutes, stirring halfway through. Meanwhile, in a small blender, combine the stock, chili powder, peanuts, sesame seeds, raisins, salt, brown sugar, oregano, cayenne, and cinnamon and purée until smooth. Pour into a small saucepan or skillet and bring to a simmer over medium heat, then cook until reduced by half, 3 to 5 minutes. Pour the hot mole sauce over the cauliflower in the pan, stir to coat, then cook until the sauce is thickened and lightly charred on the cauliflower, about 5 minutes more. Sprinkle with more sesame seeds and serve warm.

Asian Tofu Salad

Prep time: 25 minutes | Cook time: 15 minutes | Serves 2

Tofu:
1 tablespoon soy sauce
1 tablespoon vegetable oil
1 teaspoon minced fresh ginger
1 teaspoon minced garlic
230 g extra-firm tofu, drained and cubed
Salad:
60 ml rice vinegar

1 tablespoon sugar
1 teaspoon salt
1 teaspoon black pepper
25 g sliced spring onions
120 g julienned cucumber
50 g julienned red onion
130 g julienned carrots
6 butter lettuce leaves

For the tofu: In a small bowl, whisk together the soy sauce, vegetable oil, ginger, and garlic. Add the tofu and mix gently. Let stand at room temperature for 10 minutes. Arrange the tofu in a single layer in the air fryer basket. Set the air fryer to 200ºC for 15 minutes, shaking halfway through the cooking time. Meanwhile, for the salad: In a large bowl, whisk together the vinegar, sugar, salt, pepper, and spring onions. Add the cucumber, onion, and carrots and toss to combine. Set aside to marinate while the tofu cooks. To serve, arrange three lettuce leaves on each of two plates. Pile the marinated vegetables (and marinade) on the lettuce. Divide the tofu between the plates and serve.

Corn and Coriander Salad

Prep time: 10 minutes | Cook time: 10 minutes | Serves 2

2 ears of corn, shucked (halved crosswise if too large to fit in your air fryer)
1 tablespoon unsalted butter, at room temperature
1 teaspoon chili powder
¼ teaspoon garlic powder
coarse sea salt and freshly ground black pepper, to taste
20 g lightly packed fresh

coriander leaves
1 tablespoon sour cream
1 tablespoon mayonnaise
1 teaspoon adobo sauce (from a can of chipotle peppers in adobo sauce)
2 tablespoons crumbled feta cheese
Lime wedges, for serving

Brush the corn all over with the butter, then sprinkle with the chili powder and garlic powder, and season with salt and pepper. Place the corn in the air fryer and air fry at 200ºC, turning over halfway through, until the kernels are lightly charred and tender, about 10 minutes. Transfer the ears to a cutting board, let stand 1 minute, then carefully cut the kernels off the cobs and move them to a bowl. Add the coriander leaves and toss to combine (the coriander leaves will wilt slightly). In a small bowl, stir together the sour cream, mayonnaise, and adobo sauce. Divide the corn and coriander among plates and spoon the adobo dressing over the top. Sprinkle with the feta cheese and serve with lime wedges on the side.

Brussels Sprouts with Pecans and Gorgonzola

Prep time: 10 minutes | Cook time: 25 minutes | Serves 4

65 g pecans
680 g fresh Brussels sprouts, trimmed and quartered
2 tablespoons olive oil

Salt and freshly ground black pepper, to taste
30 g crumbled Gorgonzola cheese

Spread the pecans in a single layer of the air fryer and set the heat to 180ºC. Air fry for 3 to 5 minutes until the pecans are lightly browned and fragrant. Transfer the pecans to a plate and continue preheating the air fryer, increasing the heat to 200ºC. In a large bowl, toss the Brussels sprouts with the olive oil and season with salt and black pepper to taste. Working in batches if necessary, arrange the Brussels sprouts in a single layer in the air fryer basket. Pausing halfway through the baking time to shake the basket, air fry for 20 to 25 minutes until the sprouts are tender and starting to brown on the edges. Transfer the sprouts to a serving bowl and top with the toasted pecans and Gorgonzola. Serve warm or at room temperature.

Sweet-and-Sour Brussels Sprouts

Prep time: 10 minutes | Cook time: 20 minutes | Serves 2

70 g Thai sweet chili sauce
2 tablespoons black vinegar or balsamic vinegar
½ teaspoon hot sauce, such as Tabasco
230 g Brussels sprouts, trimmed (large sprouts halved)

2 small shallots, cut into ¼-inch-thick slices
coarse sea salt and freshly ground black pepper, to taste
2 teaspoons lightly packed fresh coriander leaves

In a large bowl, whisk together the chili sauce, vinegar, and hot sauce. Add the Brussels sprouts and shallots, season with salt and pepper, and toss to combine. Scrape the Brussels sprouts and sauce into a cake pan. Place the pan in the air fryer and roast at 192°C, stirring every 5 minutes, until the Brussels sprouts are tender and the sauce is reduced to a sticky glaze, about 20 minutes. Remove the pan from the air fryer and transfer the Brussels sprouts to plates. Sprinkle with the coriander and serve warm.

Chapter 6 Poultry

Chapter 6 Poultry

Chicken and Vegetable Fajitas

Prep time: 15 minutes | Cook time: 23 minutes | Serves 6

Chicken:
450 g boneless, skinless chicken thighs, cut crosswise into thirds
1 tablespoon vegetable oil
4½ teaspoons taco seasoning
Vegetables:
50 g sliced onion
150 g sliced bell pepper
1 or 2 jalapeños, quartered lengthwise

1 tablespoon vegetable oil
½ teaspoon kosher salt
½ teaspoon ground cumin
For Serving:
Tortillas
Sour cream
Shredded cheese
Guacamole
Salsa

For the chicken: In a medium bowl, toss together the chicken, vegetable oil, and taco seasoning to coat. For the vegetables: In a separate bowl, toss together the onion, bell pepper, jalapeño(s), vegetable oil, salt, and cumin to coat. Place the chicken in the air fryer basket. Set the air fryer to (190ºC for 10 minutes. Add the vegetables to the basket, toss everything together to blend the seasonings, and set the air fryer for 13 minutes more. Use a meat thermometer to ensure the chicken has reached an internal temperature of 76ºC. Transfer the chicken and vegetables to a serving platter. Serve with tortillas and the desired fajita fixings.

Thai Tacos with Peanut Sauce

Prep time: 10 minutes | Cook time: 6 minutes | Serves 4

450 g chicken mince
10 g diced onions (about 1 small onion)
2 cloves garlic, minced
¼ teaspoon fine sea salt
Sauce:
60 g creamy peanut butter, room temperature
2 tablespoons chicken broth, plus more if needed
2 tablespoons lime juice
2 tablespoons grated fresh ginger

2 tablespoons wheat-free tamari or coconut aminos
1½ teaspoons hot sauce
5 drops liquid stevia (optional)
For Serving:
2 small heads butter lettuce, leaves separated
Lime slices (optional)
For Garnish (Optional):
Coriander leaves
Shredded purple cabbage
Sliced green onions

Preheat the air fryer to 180ºC. . Place the chicken mince, onions, garlic, and salt in a pie pan or a dish that will fit in your air fryer. Break up the chicken with a spatula. Place in the air fryer and bake for 5 minutes, or until the chicken is browned and cooked through. Break up the chicken again into small crumbles. Make the sauce: In a medium-sized bowl, stir together the peanut butter, broth, lime juice, ginger, tamari, hot sauce, and stevia (if using) until well combined. If the sauce is too thick, add another tablespoon or two of broth. Taste and add more hot sauce if desired. Add half of the sauce to the pan with the chicken. Cook for another minute, until heated through, and stir well to combine. Assemble the tacos: Place several lettuce leaves on a serving plate. Place a few tablespoons of the chicken mixture in each lettuce leaf and garnish with coriander leaves, purple cabbage, and sliced green onions, if desired. Serve the remaining sauce on the side. Serve with lime slices, if desired. Store leftover meat mixture in an airtight container in the refrigerator for up to 4 days; store leftover sauce, lettuce leaves, and garnishes separately. Reheat the meat mixture in a lightly greased pie pan in a preheated 180ºC air fryer for 3 minutes, or until heated through.

Breaded Turkey Cutlets

Prep time: 5 minutes | Cook time: 8 minutes | Serves 4

60 g whole wheat bread crumbs
¼ teaspoon paprika
¼ teaspoon salt
¼ teaspoon black pepper
⅛ teaspoon dried sage

⅛ teaspoon garlic powder
1 egg
4 turkey breast cutlets
Chopped fresh parsley, for serving

Preheat the air fryer to 192ºC. In a medium shallow bowl, whisk together the bread crumbs, paprika, salt, black pepper, sage, and garlic powder. In a separate medium shallow bowl, whisk the egg until frothy. Dip each turkey cutlet into the egg mixture, then into the bread crumb mixture, coating the outside with the crumbs. Place the breaded turkey cutlets in a single layer in the bottom of the air fryer basket, making sure that they don't touch each other. Bake for 4 minutes. Turn the cutlets over, then bake for 4 minutes more, or until the internal temperature reaches 76ºC. Sprinkle on the parsley and serve.

Spice-Rubbed Chicken Thighs

Prep time: 10 minutes | Cook time: 25 minutes | Serves 4

4 (115 g) bone-in, skin-on chicken thighs
½ teaspoon salt
½ teaspoon garlic powder

2 teaspoons chili powder
1 teaspoon paprika
1 teaspoon ground cumin
1 small lime, halved

Pat chicken thighs dry and sprinkle with salt, garlic powder, chili powder, paprika, and cumin. Squeeze juice from ½ lime over thighs. Place thighs into ungreased air fryer basket. Adjust the temperature to 190ºC and roast for 25 minutes, turning thighs halfway through cooking. Thighs will be crispy and browned with an internal temperature of at least 76ºC when done. Transfer thighs to a large serving plate and drizzle with remaining lime juice. Serve warm.

South Indian Pepper Chicken

Prep time: 30 minutes | Cook time: 15 minutes | Serves 4

Spice Mix:
1 dried red chili, or ½ teaspoon dried red pepper flakes
1-inch piece cinnamon or cassia bark
1½ teaspoons coriander seeds
1 teaspoon fennel seeds
1 teaspoon cumin seeds
1 teaspoon black peppercorns
½ teaspoon cardamom seeds

¼ teaspoon ground turmeric
1 teaspoon kosher salt
Chicken:
450 g boneless, skinless chicken thighs, cut crosswise into thirds
2 medium onions, cut into ½-inch-thick slices
60 ml olive oil
Cauliflower rice, steamed rice, or naan bread, for serving

For the spice mix: Combine the dried chili, cinnamon, coriander, fennel, cumin, peppercorns, and cardamom in a clean coffee or spice grinder. Grind, shaking the grinder lightly so all the seeds and bits get into the blades, until the mixture is broken down to a fine powder. Stir in the turmeric and salt. For the chicken: Place the chicken and onions in resealable plastic bag. Add the oil and 1½ tablespoons of the spice mix. Seal the bag and massage until the chicken is well coated. Marinate at room temperature for 30 minutes or in the refrigerator for up to 24 hours. Place the chicken and onions in the air fryer basket. Set the air fryer to 180ºC for 10 minutes, stirring once halfway through the cooking time. Increase the temperature to 200ºC for 5 minutes. Use a meat thermometer to ensure the chicken has reached an internal temperature of 76ºC. Serve with steamed rice, cauliflower rice, or naan.

Piri-Piri Chicken Thighs

Prep time: 5 minutes | Cook time: 25 minutes | Serves 4

60 ml piri-piri sauce
1 tablespoon freshly squeezed lemon juice
2 tablespoons brown sugar, divided
2 cloves garlic, minced

1 tablespoon extra-virgin olive oil
4 bone-in, skin-on chicken thighs, each weighing approximately 200 to 230 g
½ teaspoon cornflour

To make the marinade, whisk together the piri-piri sauce, lemon juice, 1 tablespoon of brown sugar, and the garlic in a small bowl. While whisking, slowly pour in the oil in a steady stream and continue to whisk until emulsified. Using a skewer, poke holes in the chicken thighs and place them in a small glass dish. Pour the marinade over the chicken and turn the thighs to coat them with the sauce. Cover the dish and refrigerate for at least 15 minutes and up to 1 hour. Preheat the air fryer to 190ºC. Remove the chicken thighs from the dish, reserving the marinade, and place them skin-side down in the air fryer basket. Air fry until the internal temperature reaches 76ºC, 15 to 20 minutes. Meanwhile, whisk the remaining brown sugar and the cornflour into the marinade and microwave it on high power for 1 minute until it is bubbling and thickened to a glaze. Once the chicken is cooked, turn the thighs over and brush them with the glaze. Air fry for a few additional minutes until the glaze browns and begins to char in spots. Remove the chicken to a platter and serve with additional piri-piri sauce, if desired.

Crispy Dill Chicken Strips

Prep time: 30 minutes | Cook time: 10 minutes | Serves 4

2 whole boneless, skinless chicken breasts (about 450 g each), halved lengthwise
230 ml Italian dressing
110 g finely crushed crisps

1 tablespoon dried dill weed
1 tablespoon garlic powder
1 large egg, beaten
1 to 2 tablespoons oil

In a large resealable bag, combine the chicken and Italian dressing. Seal the bag and refrigerate to marinate at least 1 hour. In a shallow dish, stir together the potato chips, dill, and garlic powder. Place the beaten egg in a second shallow dish. Remove the chicken from the marinade. Roll the chicken pieces in the egg and the crisp mixture, coating thoroughly. Preheat the air fryer to 170ºC. Line the air fryer basket with parchment paper. Place the coated chicken on the parchment and spritz with oil. Cook for 5 minutes. Flip the chicken, spritz it with oil, and cook for 5 minutes more until the outsides are crispy and the insides are no longer pink.

Chicken Rochambeau

Prep time: 15 minutes | Cook time: 20 minutes | Serves 4

1 tablespoon butter
4 chicken tenders, cut in half crosswise
Salt and pepper, to taste
30 g flour
Oil for misting
4 slices ham, ¼- to ⅜-inches thick and large enough to cover an English muffin
2 English muffins, split

Sauce:
2 tablespoons butter
25 g chopped green onions
50 g chopped mushrooms
2 tablespoons flour
240 ml chicken broth
¼ teaspoon garlic powder
1½ teaspoons Worcestershire sauce

Place 1 tablespoon of butter in a baking pan and air fry at 200ºC for 2 minutes to melt. Sprinkle chicken tenders with salt and pepper to taste, then roll in the flour. Place chicken in baking pan, turning pieces to coat with melted butter. Air fry at 200ºC for 5 minutes. Turn chicken pieces over, and spray tops lightly with olive oil. Cook 5 minutes longer or until juices run clear. The chicken will not brown. While chicken is cooking, make the sauce: In a medium saucepan, melt the 2 tablespoons of butter. Add onions and mushrooms and sauté until tender, about 3 minutes. Stir in the flour. Gradually add broth, stirring constantly until you have a smooth gravy. Add garlic powder and Worcestershire sauce and simmer on low heat until sauce thickens, about 5 minutes. When chicken is cooked, remove baking pan from air fryer and set aside. 1Place ham slices directly into air fryer basket and air fry at 200ºC for 5 minutes or until hot and beginning to sizzle a little. Remove and set aside on top of the chicken for now. 1Place the English muffin halves in air fryer basket and air fry at 200ºC for 1 minute. 1Open air fryer and place a ham slice on top of each English muffin half. Stack 2 pieces of chicken on top of each ham slice. Air fry for 1 to 2 minutes to heat through. 1Place each English muffin stack on a serving plate and top with plenty of sauce.

Chicken Nuggets

Prep time: 10 minutes | Cook time: 15 minutes | Serves 4

450 g chicken mince thighs
110 g shredded Mozzarella cheese
1 large egg, whisked

½ teaspoon salt
¼ teaspoon dried oregano
¼ teaspoon garlic powder

In a large bowl, combine all ingredients. Form mixture into twenty nugget shapes, about 2 tablespoons each. Place nuggets into ungreased air fryer basket, working in batches if needed. Adjust the temperature to (190ºC and air fry for 15 minutes, turning nuggets halfway through cooking. Let cool 5 minutes before serving.

One-Dish Chicken and Rice

Prep time: 10 minutes | Cook time: 40 minutes | Serves 4

190 g long-grain white rice, rinsed and drained
120 g cut frozen green beans (do not thaw)
1 tablespoon minced fresh ginger

3 cloves garlic, minced
1 tablespoon toasted sesame oil
1 teaspoon kosher salt
1 teaspoon black pepper
450 g chicken wings, preferably drumettes

In a baking pan, combine the rice, green beans, ginger, garlic, sesame oil, salt, and pepper. Stir to combine. Place the chicken wings on top of the rice mixture. Cover the pan with foil. Make a long slash in the foil to allow the pan to vent steam. Place the pan in the air fryer basket. Set the air fryer to (190ºC for 30 minutes. Remove the foil. Set the air fryer to 200ºC for 10 minutes, or until the wings have browned and rendered fat into the rice and vegetables, turning the wings halfway through the cooking time.

Nashville Hot Chicken

Prep time: 20 minutes | Cook time: 24 to 28 minutes | Serves 8

1.4 kg bone-in, skin-on chicken pieces, breasts halved crosswise
1 tablespoon sea salt
1 tablespoon freshly ground black pepper
140 g finely ground blanched almond flour
130 g grated Parmesan cheese
1 tablespoon baking powder
2 teaspoons garlic powder, divided

120 g heavy (whipping) cream
2 large eggs, beaten
1 tablespoon vinegar-based hot sauce
Avocado oil spray
115 g unsalted butter
120 ml avocado oil
1 tablespoon cayenne pepper (more or less to taste)
2 tablespoons Xylitol

Sprinkle the chicken with the salt and pepper. In a large shallow bowl, whisk together the almond flour, Parmesan cheese, baking powder, and 1 teaspoon of the garlic powder. In a separate bowl, whisk together the heavy cream, eggs, and hot sauce. Dip the chicken pieces in the egg, then coat each with the almond flour mixture, pressing the mixture into the chicken to adhere. Allow

to sit for 15 minutes to let the breading set. Set the air fryer to 200ºC. Place the chicken in a single layer in the air fryer basket, being careful not to overcrowd the pieces, working in batches if necessary. Spray the chicken with oil and roast for 13 minutes. Carefully flip the chicken and spray it with more oil. Reduce the air fryer temperature to 180ºC. Roast for another 11 to 15 minutes, until an instant-read thermometer reads 70ºC. While the chicken cooks, heat the butter, avocado oil, cayenne pepper, xylitol, and remaining 1 teaspoon of garlic powder in a saucepan over medium-low heat. Cook until the butter is melted and the sugar substitute has dissolved. Remove the chicken from the air fryer. Use tongs to dip the chicken in the sauce. Place the coated chicken on a rack over a baking sheet, and allow it to rest for 5 minutes before serving.

Coconut Chicken Meatballs

Prep time: 10 minutes | Cook time: 14 minutes | Serves 4

450 g chicken mince
2 spring onions, finely chopped
20 g chopped fresh corinader leaves
20 g unsweetened shredded coconut
1 tablespoon hoisin sauce

1 tablespoon soy sauce
2 teaspoons Sriracha or other hot sauce
1 teaspoon toasted sesame oil
½ teaspoon kosher salt
1 teaspoon black pepper

In a large bowl, gently mix the chicken, spring onions, coriander, coconut, hoisin, soy sauce, Sriracha, sesame oil, salt, and pepper until thoroughly combined (the mixture will be wet and sticky). Place a sheet of parchment paper in the air fryer basket. Using a small scoop or teaspoon, drop rounds of the mixture in a single layer onto the parchment paper. Set the air fryer to 180ºC for 10 minutes, turning the meatballs halfway through the cooking time. Raise the air fryer temperature to 200ºC and cook for 4 minutes more to brown the outsides of the meatballs. Use a meat thermometer to ensure the meatballs have reached an internal temperature of 76ºC. Transfer the meatballs to a serving platter. Repeat with any remaining chicken mixture.

Chicken Patties

Prep time: 15 minutes | Cook time: 12 minutes | Serves 4

450 g chicken thigh mince
110 g shredded Mozzarella cheese
1 teaspoon dried parsley

½ teaspoon garlic powder
¼ teaspoon onion powder
1 large egg
60 g pork rinds, finely ground

In a large bowl, mix chicken mince, Mozzarella, parsley, garlic powder, and onion powder. Form into four patties. Place patties in the freezer for 15 to 20 minutes until they begin to firm up. Whisk egg in a medium bowl. Place the ground pork rinds into a large bowl. Dip each chicken patty into the egg and then press into pork rinds to fully coat. Place patties into the air fryer basket. Adjust the temperature to 180ºC and air fry for 12 minutes. Patties will be firm and cooked to an internal temperature of 76ºC when done. Serve immediately.

Bacon-Wrapped Chicken Breasts Rolls

Prep time: 10 minutes | Cook time: 15 minutes | Serves 4

15 g chopped fresh chives
2 tablespoons lemon juice
1 teaspoon dried sage
1 teaspoon fresh rosemary leaves
15 g fresh parsley leaves
4 cloves garlic, peeled
1 teaspoon ground fennel
3 teaspoons sea salt

½ teaspoon red pepper flakes
4 (115 g) boneless, skinless chicken breasts, pounded to ¼ inch thick
8 slices bacon
Sprigs of fresh rosemary, for garnish
Cooking spray

Preheat the air fryer to 170ºC. Spritz the air fryer basket with cooking spray. Put the chives, lemon juice, sage, rosemary, parsley, garlic, fennel, salt, and red pepper flakes in a food processor, then pulse to purée until smooth. Unfold the chicken breasts on a clean work surface, then brush the top side of the chicken breasts with the sauce. Roll the chicken breasts up from the shorter side, then wrap each chicken rolls with 2 bacon slices to cover. Secure with toothpicks. Arrange the rolls in the preheated air fryer, then cook for 10 minutes. Flip the rolls halfway through. Increase the heat to 200ºC and air fry for 5 more minutes or until the bacon is browned and crispy. Transfer the rolls to a large plate. Discard the toothpicks and spread with rosemary sprigs before serving.

Chicken Breasts with Asparagus, Beans, and Rocket

Prep time: 20 minutes | Cook time: 25 minutes | Serves 2

160 g canned cannellini beans, rinsed
1½ tablespoons red wine vinegar
1 garlic clove, minced
2 tablespoons extra-virgin olive oil, divided
Salt and ground black pepper, to taste

½ red onion, sliced thinly
230 g asparagus, trimmed and cut into 1-inch lengths
2 (230 g) boneless, skinless chicken breasts, trimmed
¼ teaspoon paprika
½ teaspoon ground coriander
60 g baby rocket, rinsed and drained

Preheat the air fryer to 200ºC. Warm the beans in microwave for 1 minutes and combine with red wine vinegar, garlic, 1 tablespoon of olive oil, ¼ teaspoon of salt, and ¼ teaspoon of ground black pepper in a bowl. Stir to mix well. Combine the onion with ⅛ teaspoon of salt, ⅛ teaspoon of ground black pepper, and 2 teaspoons of olive oil in a separate bowl. Toss to coat well. Place the onion in the air fryer and air fry for 2 minutes, then add the asparagus and air fry for 8 more minutes or until the asparagus is tender. Shake the basket halfway through. Transfer the onion and asparagus to the bowl with beans. Set aside. Toss the chicken breasts with remaining ingredients, except for the baby rocket, in a large bowl. Put the chicken breasts in the air fryer and air fry for 14 minutes or until the internal temperature of the chicken reaches at least 76ºC. Flip the breasts halfway through. Remove the chicken from the air fryer and serve on an aluminum foil with asparagus, beans, onion, and rocket. Sprinkle with salt and ground black pepper. Toss to serve.

Korean Honey Wings

Prep time: 10 minutes | Cook time: 25 minutes per batch | Serves 4

55 g gochujang, or red pepper paste
55 g mayonnaise
2 tablespoons honey
1 tablespoon sesame oil
2 teaspoons minced garlic
1 tablespoon sugar

2 teaspoons ground ginger
1.4 kg whole chicken wings
Olive oil spray
1 teaspoon salt
½ teaspoon freshly ground black pepper

In a large bowl, whisk the gochujang, mayonnaise, honey, sesame oil, garlic, sugar, and ginger. Set aside. Insert the crisper plate into the basket and the basket into the unit. Preheat the unit by selecting AIR FRY, setting the temperature to 200ºC, and setting the time to 3 minutes. Select START/STOP to begin. To prepare the chicken wings, cut the wings in half. The meatier part is the drumette. Cut off and discard the wing tip from the flat part (or save the wing tips in the freezer to make chicken stock). Once the unit is preheated, spray the crisper plate with olive oil. Working in batches, place half the chicken wings into the basket, spray them with olive oil, and sprinkle with the salt and pepper. Select AIR FRY, set the temperature to 200ºC, and set the time to 20 minutes. Select START/STOP to begin. After 10 minutes, remove the basket, flip the wings, and spray them with more olive oil. Reinsert the basket to resume cooking. Cook the wings to an internal temperature of 76ºC, then transfer them to the bowl with the prepared sauce and toss to coat. Repeat steps 4, 5, 6, and 7 for the remaining chicken wings. Return the coated wings to the basket and air fry for 4 to 6 minutes more until the sauce has glazed the wings and the chicken is crisp. After 3 minutes, check the wings to make sure they aren't burning. Serve hot.

Barbecued Chicken with Creamy Coleslaw

Prep time: 10 minutes | Cook time: 20 minutes | Serves 2

270 g shredded coleslaw mix
Salt and pepper
2 (340 g) bone-in split chicken breasts, trimmed
1 teaspoon vegetable oil
2 tablespoons barbecue sauce,

plus extra for serving
2 tablespoons mayonnaise
2 tablespoons sour cream
1 teaspoon distilled white vinegar, plus extra for seasoning
¼ teaspoon sugar

Preheat the air fryer to 180ºC. Toss coleslaw mix and ¼ teaspoon salt in a colander set over bowl. Let sit until wilted slightly, about 30 minutes. Rinse, drain, and dry well with a dish towel. Meanwhile, pat chicken dry with paper towels, rub with oil, and season with salt and pepper. Arrange breasts skin-side down in air fryer basket, spaced evenly apart, alternating ends. Bake for 10 minutes. Flip breasts and brush skin side with barbecue sauce. Return basket to air fryer and bake until well browned and chicken registers 70ºC, 10 to 15 minutes. Transfer chicken to serving platter, tent loosely with aluminum foil, and let rest for 5 minutes. While chicken rests, whisk mayonnaise, sour cream, vinegar, sugar, and pinch pepper together in a large bowl. Stir in coleslaw mix and season with salt, pepper, and additional vinegar to taste. Serve chicken with coleslaw, passing extra barbecue sauce separately.

Chicken and Gruyère Cordon Bleu

Prep time: 15 minutes | Cook time: 15 minutes | Serves 4

4 chicken breast filets
75 g chopped ham
75 g grated Swiss cheese, or Gruyère cheese
30 g all-purpose flour
Pinch salt
Freshly ground black pepper, to taste
½ teaspoon dried marjoram
1 egg
120 g panko bread crumbs
Olive oil spray

Put the chicken breast filets on a work surface and gently press them with the palm of your hand to make them a bit thinner. Don't tear the meat. In a small bowl, combine the ham and cheese. Divide this mixture among the chicken filets. Wrap the chicken around the filling to enclose it, using toothpicks to hold the chicken together. In a shallow bowl, stir together the flour, salt, pepper, and marjoram. In another bowl, beat the egg. Spread the panko on a plate. Dip the chicken in the flour mixture, in the egg, and in the panko to coat thoroughly. Press the crumbs into the chicken so they stick well. Insert the crisper plate into the basket and the basket into the unit. Preheat the unit by selecting BAKE, setting the temperature to 190ºC, and setting the time to 3 minutes. Select START/STOP to begin. Once the unit is preheated, spray the crisper plate with olive oil. Place the chicken into the basket and spray it with olive oil. Select BAKE, set the temperature to 190ºC, and set the time to 15 minutes. Select START/STOP to begin. 1When the cooking is complete, the chicken should be cooked through and a food thermometer inserted into the chicken should register 76ºC. Carefully remove the toothpicks and serve.

Thai Chicken with Cucumber and Chili Salad

Prep time: 25 minutes | Cook time: 25 minutes | Serves 6

2 (570 g) small chickens, giblets discarded
1 tablespoon fish sauce
6 tablespoons chopped fresh coriander
2 teaspoons lime zest
1 teaspoon ground coriander
2 garlic cloves, minced
2 tablespoons packed light brown sugar
2 teaspoons vegetable oil
Salt and ground black pepper, to taste
1 English cucumber, halved lengthwise and sliced thin
1 Thai chili, stemmed, deseeded, and minced
2 tablespoons chopped dry-roasted peanuts
1 small shallot, sliced thinly
1 tablespoon lime juice
Lime wedges, for serving
Cooking spray

Arrange a chicken on a clean work surface, remove the backbone with kitchen shears, then pound the chicken breast to flat. Cut the breast in half. Repeat with the remaining chicken. Loose the breast and thigh skin with your fingers, then pat the chickens dry and pierce about 10 holes into the fat deposits of the chickens. Tuck the wings under the chickens. Combine 2 teaspoons of fish sauce, coriander, lime zest, coriander, garlic, 4 teaspoons of sugar, 1 teaspoon of vegetable oil, ½ teaspoon of salt, and ⅛ teaspoon of ground black pepper in a small bowl. Stir to mix well. Rub the fish sauce mixture under the breast and thigh skin of the game chickens,

then let sit for 10 minutes to marinate. Preheat the air fryer to 200ºC. Spritz the air fryer basket with cooking spray. Arrange the marinated chickens in the preheated air fryer, skin side down. Air fry for 15 minutes, then gently turn the game hens over and air fry for 10 more minutes or until the skin is golden brown and the internal temperature of the chickens reads at least 76ºC. Meanwhile, combine all the remaining ingredients, except for the lime wedges, in a large bowl and sprinkle with salt and black pepper. Toss to mix well. Transfer the fried chickens on a large plate, then sit the salad aside and squeeze the lime wedges over before serving.

Thai-Style Cornish Game Hens

Prep time: 30 minutes | Cook time: 20 minutes | Serves 4

20 g chopped fresh coriander leaves and stems
60 ml fish sauce
1 tablespoon soy sauce
1 serrano chili, seeded and chopped
8 garlic cloves, smashed
2 tablespoons sugar
2 tablespoons lemongrass paste
2 teaspoons black pepper
2 teaspoons ground coriander
1 teaspoon kosher salt
1 teaspoon ground turmeric
2 Cornish game hens, giblets removed, split in half lengthwise

In a blender, combine the coriander, fish sauce, soy sauce, serrano, garlic, sugar, lemongrass, black pepper, coriander, salt, and turmeric. Blend until smooth. Place the game hen halves in a large bowl. Pour the coriander mixture over the hen halves and toss to coat. Marinate at room temperature for 30 minutes, or cover and refrigerate for up to 24 hours. Arrange the hen halves in a single layer in the air fryer basket. Set the air fryer to 200ºC for 20 minutes. Use a meat thermometer to ensure the game hens have reached an internal temperature of 76ºC.

Chicken with Lettuce

Prep time: 15 minutes | Cook time: 14 minutes | Serves 4

450 g chicken breast tenders, chopped into bite-size pieces
½ onion, thinly sliced
½ red bell pepper, seeded and thinly sliced
½ green bell pepper, seeded and thinly sliced
1 tablespoon olive oil
1 tablespoon fajita seasoning
1 teaspoon kosher salt
Juice of ½ lime
8 large lettuce leaves
230 g prepared guacamole

Preheat the air fryer to 200ºC. In a large bowl, combine the chicken, onion, and peppers. Drizzle with the olive oil and toss until thoroughly coated. Add the fajita seasoning and salt and toss again. Working in batches if necessary, arrange the chicken and vegetables in a single layer in the air fryer basket. Pausing halfway through the cooking time to shake the basket, air fry for 14 minutes, or until the vegetables are tender and a thermometer inserted into the thickest piece of chicken registers 76ºC. Transfer the mixture to a serving platter and drizzle with the fresh lime juice. Serve with the lettuce leaves and top with the guacamole.

Pomegranate-Glazed Chicken with Couscous Salad

Prep time: 25 minutes | Cook time: 20 minutes | Serves 4

3 tablespoons plus 2 teaspoons pomegranate molasses
½ teaspoon ground cinnamon
1 teaspoon minced fresh thyme
Salt and ground black pepper, to taste
2 (340 g) bone-in split chicken breasts, trimmed
60 ml chicken broth
60 ml water
80 g couscous
1 tablespoon minced fresh parsley
60 g cherry tomatoes, quartered
1 scallion, white part minced, green part sliced thin on bias
1 tablespoon extra-virgin olive oil
30 g feta cheese, crumbled
Cooking spray

Preheat the air fryer to 180°C. Spritz the air fryer basket with cooking spray. Combine 3 tablespoons of pomegranate molasses, cinnamon, thyme, and ⅛ teaspoon of salt in a small bowl. Stir to mix well. Set aside. Place the chicken breasts in the preheated air fryer, skin side down, and spritz with cooking spray. Sprinkle with salt and ground black pepper. Air fry the chicken for 10 minutes, then brush the chicken with half of pomegranate molasses mixture and flip. Air fry for 5 more minutes. Brush the chicken with remaining pomegranate molasses mixture and flip. Air fry for another 5 minutes or until the internal temperature of the chicken breasts reaches at least 76°C. Meanwhile, pour the broth and water in a pot and bring to a boil over medium-high heat. Add the couscous and sprinkle with salt. Cover and simmer for 7 minutes or until the liquid is almost absorbed. Combine the remaining ingredients, except for the cheese, with cooked couscous in a large bowl. Toss to mix well. Scatter with the feta cheese. When the air frying is complete, remove the chicken from the air fryer and allow to cool for 10 minutes. Serve with vegetable and couscous salad.

Buttermilk-Fried Drumsticks

Prep time: 10 minutes | Cook time: 25 minutes | Serves 2

1 egg
120 g buttermilk
90 g self-rising flour
90 g seasoned panko bread crumbs
1 teaspoon salt
¼ teaspoon ground black pepper (to mix into coating)
4 chicken drumsticks, skin on
Oil for misting or cooking spray

Beat together egg and buttermilk in shallow dish. In a second shallow dish, combine the flour, panko crumbs, salt, and pepper. Sprinkle chicken legs with additional salt and pepper to taste. Dip legs in buttermilk mixture, then roll in panko mixture, pressing in crumbs to make coating stick. Mist with oil or cooking spray. Spray the air fryer basket with cooking spray. Cook drumsticks at 180°C for 10 minutes. Turn pieces over and cook an additional 10 minutes. Turn pieces to check for browning. If you have any white spots that haven't begun to brown, spritz them with oil or cooking spray. Continue cooking for 5 more minutes or until crust is golden brown and juices run clear. Larger, meatier drumsticks will take longer to cook than small ones.

Peanut Butter Chicken Satay

Prep time: 12 minutes | Cook time: 12 to 18 minutes | Serves 4

120 g crunchy peanut butter
80 ml chicken broth
3 tablespoons low-sodium soy sauce
2 tablespoons freshly squeezed lemon juice
2 garlic cloves, minced
2 tablespoons extra-virgin olive oil
1 teaspoon curry powder
450 g chicken tenders
Cooking oil spray

In a medium bowl, whisk the peanut butter, broth, soy sauce, lemon juice, garlic, olive oil, and curry powder until smooth. Place 2 tablespoons of this mixture into a small bowl. Transfer the remaining sauce to a serving bowl and set aside. Add the chicken tenders to the bowl with the 2 tablespoons of sauce and stir to coat. Let stand for a few minutes to marinate. Insert the crisper plate into the basket and the basket into the unit. Preheat the unit by selecting AIR FRY, setting the temperature to 200°C, and setting the time to 3 minutes. Select START/STOP to begin. Run a 6-inch bamboo skewer lengthwise through each chicken tender. Once the unit is preheated, spray the crisper plate with cooking oil. Working in batches, place half the chicken skewers into the basket in a single layer without overlapping. Select AIR FRY, set the temperature to 200°C, and set the time to 9 minutes. Select START/STOP to begin. After 6 minutes, check the chicken. If a food thermometer inserted into the chicken registers 76°C, it is done. If not, resume cooking. Repeat steps 6, 7, and 8 with the remaining chicken. 1When the cooking is complete, serve the chicken with the reserved sauce.

Gochujang Chicken Wings

Prep time: 15 minutes | Cook time: 25 minutes | Serves 4

Wings:
900 g chicken wings
1 teaspoon kosher salt
1 teaspoon black pepper or gochugaru (Korean red pepper)
Sauce:
2 tablespoons gochujang (Korean chili paste)
1 tablespoon mayonnaise
1 tablespoon toasted sesame oil
1 tablespoon minced fresh ginger
1 tablespoon minced garlic
1 teaspoon sugar
1 teaspoon agave nectar or honey
For Serving
1 teaspoon sesame seeds
25 g chopped spring onions

For the wings: Season the wings with the salt and pepper and place in the air fryer basket. Set the air fryer to 200°C for 20 minutes, turning the wings halfway through the cooking time. Meanwhile, for the sauce: In a small bowl, combine the gochujang, mayonnaise, sesame oil, ginger, garlic, sugar, and agave; set aside. As you near the 20-minute mark, use a meat thermometer to check the meat. When the wings reach 70°C, transfer them to a large bowl. Pour about half the sauce on the wings; toss to coat (serve the remaining sauce as a dip). Return the wings to the air fryer basket and cook for 5 minutes, until the sauce has glazed. Transfer the wings to a serving platter. Sprinkle with the sesame seeds and spring onions. Serve with the reserved sauce on the side for dipping.

Chicken Croquettes with Creole Sauce

Prep time: 30 minutes | Cook time: 10 minutes | Serves 4

280 g shredded cooked chicken	Creole Sauce:
120 g shredded Cheddar cheese	60 g mayonnaise
2 eggs	60 g sour cream
15 g finely chopped onion	1½ teaspoons Dijon mustard
25 g almond meal	1½ teaspoons fresh lemon juice
1 tablespoon poultry seasoning	½ teaspoon garlic powder
Olive oil	½ teaspoon Creole seasoning

In a large bowl, combine the chicken, Cheddar, eggs, onion, almond meal, and poultry seasoning. Stir gently until thoroughly combined. Cover and refrigerate for 30 minutes. Meanwhile, to make the Creole sauce: In a small bowl, whisk together the mayonnaise, sour cream, Dijon mustard, lemon juice, garlic powder, and Creole seasoning until thoroughly combined. Cover and refrigerate until ready to serve. Preheat the air fryer to 200ºC. Divide the chicken mixture into 8 portions and shape into patties. Working in batches if necessary, arrange the patties in a single layer in the air fryer basket and coat both sides lightly with olive oil. Pausing halfway through the cooking time to flip the patties, air fry for 10 minutes, or until lightly browned and the cheese is melted. Serve with the Creole sauce.

Coconut Chicken Wings with Mango Sauce

Prep time: 15 minutes | Cook time: 20 minutes | Serves 4

16 chicken drumettes (party wings)	coconut
60 ml full-fat coconut milk	60 g all-purpose flour
1 tablespoon sriracha	Cooking oil spray
1 teaspoon onion powder	165 g mango, cut into ½-inch chunks
1 teaspoon garlic powder	15 g fresh coriander, chopped
Salt and freshly ground black pepper, to taste	25 g red onion, chopped
25 g shredded unsweetened	2 garlic cloves, minced
	Juice of ½ lime

Place the drumettes in a resealable plastic bag. In a small bowl, whisk the coconut milk and sriracha. Drizzle the drumettes with the sriracha–coconut milk mixture. Season the drumettes with the onion powder, garlic powder, salt, and pepper. Seal the bag. Shake it thoroughly to combine the seasonings and coat the chicken. Marinate for at least 30 minutes, preferably overnight, in the refrigerator. When the drumettes are almost done marinating, in a large bowl, stir together the shredded coconut and flour. Dip the drumettes into the coconut-flour mixture. Press the flour mixture onto the chicken with your hands. Insert the crisper plate into the basket and the basket into the unit. Preheat the unit by selecting AIR FRY, setting the temperature to 200ºC, and setting the time to 3 minutes. Select START/STOP to begin. Once the unit is preheated, spray the crisper plate and the basket with cooking oil. Place the drumettes in the air fryer. It is okay to stack them. Spray the drumettes with cooking oil, being sure to cover the bottom layer. Select AIR FRY, set the temperature to 200ºC, and set the time to 20 minutes. Select START/STOP to begin. After 5 minutes, remove the basket and shake it to ensure all pieces cook through. Reinsert the basket to resume cooking. Remove and shake the basket every 5 minutes, twice more, until a food thermometer inserted into the drumettes registers 76ºC. 1When the cooking is complete, let the chicken cool for 5 minutes. 1While the chicken cooks and cools, make the salsa. In a small bowl, combine the mango, coriander, red onion, garlic, and lime juice. Mix well until fully combined. Serve with the wings.

Crunchy Chicken Tenders

Prep time: 5 minutes | Cook time: 12 minutes | Serves 4

1 egg	½ teaspoon dried thyme
60 ml unsweetened almond milk	½ teaspoon dried sage
30 g whole wheat flour	½ teaspoon garlic powder
30 g whole wheat bread crumbs	450 g chicken tenderloins
½ teaspoon salt	1 lemon, quartered
½ teaspoon black pepper	

Preheat the air fryer to 184ºC. In a shallow bowl, beat together the egg and almond milk until frothy. In a separate shallow bowl, whisk together the flour, bread crumbs, salt, pepper, thyme, sage, and garlic powder. Dip each chicken tenderloin into the egg mixture, then into the bread crumb mixture, coating the outside with the crumbs. Place the breaded chicken tenderloins into the bottom of the air fryer basket in an even layer, making sure that they don't touch each other. Cook for 6 minutes, then turn and cook for an additional 5 to 6 minutes. Serve with lemon slices.

Tex-Mex Chicken Roll-Ups

Prep time: 10 minutes | Cook time: 14 to 17 minutes | Serves 8

900 g boneless, skinless chicken breasts or thighs	black pepper, to taste
1 teaspoon chili powder	170 g Monterey Jack cheese, shredded
½ teaspoon smoked paprika	115 g canned diced green chilies
½ teaspoon ground cumin	Avocado oil spray
Sea salt and freshly ground	

Place the chicken in a large zip-top bag or between two pieces of plastic wrap. Using a meat mallet or heavy skillet, pound the chicken until it is about ¼ inch thick. In a small bowl, combine the chili powder, smoked paprika, cumin, and salt and pepper to taste. Sprinkle both sides of the chicken with the seasonings. Sprinkle the chicken with the Monterey Jack cheese, then the diced green chilies. Roll up each piece of chicken from the long side, tucking in the ends as you go. Secure the roll-up with a toothpick. Set the air fryer to 180ºC. . Spray the outside of the chicken with avocado oil. Place the chicken in a single layer in the basket, working in batches if necessary, and roast for 7 minutes. Flip and cook for another 7 to 10 minutes, until an instant-read thermometer reads 70ºC. Remove the chicken from the air fryer and allow it to rest for about 5 minutes before serving.

Thai Curry Meatballs

Prep time: 10 minutes | Cook time: 10 minutes | Serves 4

450 g chicken mince
15 g chopped fresh coriander
1 teaspoon chopped fresh mint
1 tablespoon fresh lime juice
1 tablespoon Thai red, green, or yellow curry paste
1 tablespoon fish sauce
2 garlic cloves, minced
2 teaspoons minced fresh ginger
½ teaspoon kosher salt
½ teaspoon black pepper
¼ teaspoon red pepper flakes

Preheat the air fryer to 200ºC. In a large bowl, gently mix the chicken mince, coriander, mint, lime juice, curry paste, fish sauce, garlic, ginger, salt, black pepper, and red pepper flakes until thoroughly combined. Form the mixture into 16 meatballs. Place the meatballs in a single layer in the air fryer basket. Air fry for 10 minutes, turning the meatballs halfway through the cooking time. Use a meat thermometer to ensure the meatballs have reached an internal temperature of 76ºC. Serve immediately.

Spanish Chicken and Mini Sweet Pepper Baguette

Prep time: 10 minutes | Cook time: 20 minutes | Serves 2

570 g assorted small chicken parts, breasts cut into halves
¼ teaspoon salt
¼ teaspoon ground black pepper
2 teaspoons olive oil
230 g mini sweet peppers
60 g light mayonnaise
¼ teaspoon smoked paprika
½ clove garlic, crushed
Baguette, for serving
Cooking spray

Preheat air fryer to 190ºC. Spritz the air fryer basket with cooking spray. Toss the chicken with salt, ground black pepper, and olive oil in a large bowl. Arrange the sweet peppers and chicken in the preheated air fryer and air fry for 10 minutes, then transfer the peppers on a plate. Flip the chicken and air fry for 10 more minutes or until well browned. Meanwhile, combine the mayo, paprika, and garlic in a small bowl. Stir to mix well. Assemble the baguette with chicken and sweet pepper, then spread with mayo mixture and serve.

African Merguez Meatballs

Prep time: 30 minutes | Cook time: 10 minutes | Serves 4

450 g chicken mince
2 garlic cloves, finely minced
1 tablespoon sweet Hungarian paprika
1 teaspoon kosher salt
1 teaspoon sugar
1 teaspoon ground cumin
½ teaspoon black pepper
½ teaspoon ground fennel
½ teaspoon ground coriander
½ teaspoon cayenne pepper
¼ teaspoon ground allspice

In a large bowl, gently mix the chicken, garlic, paprika, salt, sugar,

cumin, black pepper, fennel, coriander, cayenne, and allspice until all the ingredients are incorporated. Let stand for 30 minutes at room temperature, or cover and refrigerate for up to 24 hours. Form the mixture into 16 meatballs. Arrange them in a single layer in the air fryer basket. Set the air fryer to 200ºC for 10 minutes, turning the meatballs halfway through the cooking time. Use a meat thermometer to ensure the meatballs have reached an internal temperature of 76ºC.

Lemon Thyme Roasted Chicken

Prep time: 10 minutes | Cook time: 60 minutes | Serves 6

2 tablespoons baking powder
1 teaspoon smoked paprika
Sea salt and freshly ground black pepper, to taste
900 g chicken wings or chicken drumettes
Avocado oil spray
80 ml avocado oil
120 ml Buffalo hot sauce, such as Frank's RedHot
4 tablespoons unsalted butter
2 tablespoons apple cider vinegar
1 teaspoon minced garlic

In a large bowl, stir together the baking powder, smoked paprika, and salt and pepper to taste. Add the chicken wings and toss to coat. Set the air fryer to 200ºC. Spray the wings with oil. Place the wings in the basket in a single layer, working in batches, and air fry for 20 to 25 minutes. Check with an instant-read thermometer and remove when they reach 70ºC. Let rest until they reach 76ºC. While the wings are cooking, whisk together the avocado oil, hot sauce, butter, vinegar, and garlic in a small saucepan over medium-low heat until warm. When the wings are done cooking, toss them with the Buffalo sauce. Serve warm.

Turkey Meatloaf

Prep time: 10 minutes | Cook time: 50 minutes | Serves 4

230 g sliced mushrooms
1 small onion, coarsely chopped
2 cloves garlic
680 g 85% lean turkey mince
2 eggs, lightly beaten
1 tablespoon tomato paste
25 g almond meal
2 tablespoons almond milk
1 tablespoon dried oregano
1 teaspoon salt
½ teaspoon freshly ground black pepper
1 Roma tomato, thinly sliced

Preheat the air fryer to 180ºC. . Lightly coat a round pan with olive oil and set aside. In a food processor fitted with a metal blade, combine the mushrooms, onion, and garlic. Pulse until finely chopped. Transfer the vegetables to a large mixing bowl. Add the turkey, eggs, tomato paste, almond meal, milk, oregano, salt, and black pepper. Mix gently until thoroughly combined. Transfer the mixture to the prepared pan and shape into a loaf. Arrange the tomato slices on top. Air fry for 50 minutes or until the meatloaf is nicely browned and a thermometer inserted into the thickest part registers 76ºC. Remove from the air fryer and let rest for about 10 minutes before slicing.

Easy Cajun Chicken Drumsticks

Prep time: 5 minutes | Cook time: 40 minutes | Serves 5

1 tablespoon olive oil
10 chicken drumsticks
1½ tablespoons Cajun seasoning

Salt and ground black pepper, to taste

Preheat the air fryer to 200ºC. Grease the air fryer basket with olive oil. On a clean work surface, rub the chicken drumsticks with Cajun seasoning, salt, and ground black pepper. Arrange the seasoned chicken drumsticks in a single layer in the air fryer. You need to work in batches to avoid overcrowding. Air fry for 18 minutes or until lightly browned. Flip the drumsticks halfway through. Remove the chicken drumsticks from the air fryer. Serve immediately.

Chicken Drumsticks with Barbecue-Honey Sauce

Prep time: 5 minutes | Cook time: 40 minutes | Serves 5

1 tablespoon olive oil
10 chicken drumsticks
Chicken seasoning or rub, to taste

Salt and ground black pepper, to taste
240 ml barbecue sauce
85 g honey

Preheat the air fryer to 200ºC. Grease the air fryer basket with olive oil. Rub the chicken drumsticks with chicken seasoning or rub, salt and ground black pepper on a clean work surface. Arrange the chicken drumsticks in a single layer in the air fryer, then air fry for 18 minutes or until lightly browned. Flip the drumsticks halfway through. You may need to work in batches to avoid overcrowding. Meanwhile, combine the barbecue sauce and honey in a small bowl. Stir to mix well. Remove the drumsticks from the air fryer and baste with the sauce mixture to serve.

Pork Rind Fried Chicken

Prep time: 30 minutes | Cook time: 20 minutes | Serves 4

60 ml buffalo sauce
4 (115 g) boneless, skinless chicken breasts
½ teaspoon paprika

½ teaspoon garlic powder
¼ teaspoon ground black pepper
60 g g plain pork rinds, finely crushed

Pour buffalo sauce into a large sealable bowl or bag. Add chicken and toss to coat. Place sealed bowl or bag into refrigerator and let marinate at least 30 minutes up to overnight. Remove chicken from marinade but do not shake excess sauce off chicken. Sprinkle both sides of thighs with paprika, garlic powder, and pepper. Place pork rinds into a large bowl and press each chicken breast into pork rinds to coat evenly on both sides. Place chicken into ungreased air fryer basket. Adjust the temperature to 200ºC and roast for 20 minutes, turning chicken halfway through cooking. Chicken will be golden and have an internal temperature of at least 76ºC when done. Serve warm.

Air Fried Chicken Potatoes with Sun-Dried Tomato

Prep time: 15 minutes | Cook time: 25 minutes | Serves 2

2 teaspoons minced fresh oregano, divided
2 teaspoons minced fresh thyme, divided
2 teaspoons extra-virgin olive oil, plus extra as needed
450 g fingerling potatoes, unpeeled
2 (340 g) bone-in split chicken breasts, trimmed
1 garlic clove, minced

15 g oil-packed sun-dried tomatoes, patted dry and chopped
1½ tablespoons red wine vinegar
1 tablespoon capers, rinsed and minced
1 small shallot, minced
Salt and ground black pepper, to taste

Preheat the air fryer to 180ºC. Combine 1 teaspoon of oregano, 1 teaspoon of thyme, ¼ teaspoon of salt, ¼ teaspoon of ground black pepper, 1 teaspoons of olive oil in a large bowl. Add the potatoes and toss to coat well. Combine the chicken with remaining thyme, oregano, and olive oil. Sprinkle with garlic, salt, and pepper. Toss to coat well. Place the potatoes in the preheated air fryer, then arrange the chicken on top of the potatoes. Air fry for 25 minutes or until the internal temperature of the chicken reaches at least 76ºC and the potatoes are wilted. Flip the chicken and potatoes halfway through. Meanwhile, combine the sun-dried tomatoes, vinegar, capers, and shallot in a separate large bowl. Sprinkle with salt and ground black pepper. Toss to mix well. Remove the chicken and potatoes from the air fryer and allow to cool for 10 minutes. Serve with the sun-dried tomato mix.

Smoky Chicken Leg Quarters

Prep time: 30 minutes | Cook time: 23 to 27 minutes | Serves 6

120 ml avocado oil
2 teaspoons smoked paprika
1 teaspoon sea salt
1 teaspoon garlic powder
½ teaspoon dried rosemary

½ teaspoon dried thyme
½ teaspoon freshly ground black pepper
900 g bone-in, skin-on chicken leg quarters

In a blender or small bowl, combine the avocado oil, smoked paprika, salt, garlic powder, rosemary, thyme, and black pepper. Place the chicken in a shallow dish or large zip-top bag. Pour the marinade over the chicken, making sure all the legs are coated. Cover and marinate for at least 2 hours or overnight. Place the chicken in a single layer in the air fryer basket, working in batches if necessary. Set the air fryer to 200ºC and air fry for 15 minutes. Flip the chicken legs, then reduce the temperature to 180ºC. . Cook for 8 to 12 minutes more, until an instant-read thermometer reads 70ºC when inserted into the thickest piece of chicken. Allow to rest for 5 to 10 minutes before serving.

Chicken Schnitzel

Prep time: 15 minutes | Cook time: 5 minutes | Serves 4

60 g all-purpose flour
1 teaspoon marjoram
½ teaspoon thyme
1 teaspoon dried parsley flakes
½ teaspoon salt
1 egg

1 teaspoon lemon juice
1 teaspoon water
120 g breadcrumbs
4 chicken tenders, pounded thin, cut in half lengthwise
Cooking spray

Preheat the air fryer to 200ºC and spritz with cooking spray. Combine the flour, marjoram, thyme, parsley, and salt in a shallow dish. Stir to mix well. Whisk the egg with lemon juice and water in a large bowl. Pour the breadcrumbs in a separate shallow dish. Roll the chicken halves in the flour mixture first, then in the egg mixture, and then roll over the breadcrumbs to coat well. Shake the excess off. Arrange the chicken halves in the preheated air fryer and spritz with cooking spray on both sides. Air fry for 5 minutes or until the chicken halves are golden brown and crispy. Flip the halves halfway through. Serve immediately.

Chapter 7 Beef, Pork, and Lamb

Chapter 7 Beef, Pork, and Lamb

Currywurst

Prep time: 15 minutes | Cook time: 12 minutes | Serves 4

235 ml tomato sauce
2 tablespoons cider vinegar
2 teaspoons curry powder
2 teaspoons sweet paprika
1 teaspoon sugar

¼ teaspoon cayenne pepper
1 small onion, diced
450 g bratwurst, sliced diagonally into 1-inch pieces

In a large bowl, combine the tomato sauce, vinegar, curry powder, paprika, sugar, and cayenne. Whisk until well combined. Stir in the onion and bratwurst. Transfer the mixture to a baking pan. Place the pan in the air fryer basket. Set the air fryer to 204ºC for 12 minutes, or until the sausage is heated through and the sauce is bubbling.

Pork Schnitzels with Sour Cream and Dill Sauce

Prep time: 5 minutes | Cook time: 24 minutes | Serves 4 to 6

120 ml flour
1½ teaspoons salt
Freshly ground black pepper, to taste
2 eggs
120 ml milk
355 ml toasted breadcrumbs
1 teaspoon paprika
6 boneless pork chops (about 680 g), fat trimmed, pound to ½-inch thick

2 tablespoons olive oil
3 tablespoons melted butter
Lemon wedges, for serving
Sour Cream and Dill Sauce:
235 ml chicken stock
1½ tablespoons cornflour
80 ml sour cream
1½ tablespoons chopped fresh dill
Salt and ground black pepper, to taste

Preheat the air fryer to 204ºC. Combine the flour with salt and black pepper in a large bowl. Stir to mix well. Whisk the egg with milk in a second bowl. Stir the breadcrumbs and paprika in a third bowl. Dredge the pork chops in the flour bowl, then in the egg milk, and then into the breadcrumbs bowl. Press to coat well. Shake the excess off. Arrange one pork chop in the preheated air fryer each time, then brush with olive oil and butter on all sides. Air fry each pork chop for 4 minutes or until golden brown and crispy. Flip the chop halfway through the cooking time. Transfer the cooked pork chop (schnitzel) to a baking pan in the oven and keep warm over low heat while air frying the remaining pork chops. Meanwhile, combine the chicken stock and cornflour in a small saucepan and bring to a boil over medium-high heat. Simmer for 2 more minutes. Turn off the heat, then mix in the sour cream, fresh dill, salt, and black pepper. Remove the schnitzels from the air fryer to a plate and baste with sour cream and dill sauce. Squeeze the lemon wedges over and slice to serve.

Goat Cheese-Stuffed Bavette Steak

Prep time: 10 minutes | Cook time: 14 minutes | Serves 6

450 g bavette or skirt steak
1 tablespoon avocado oil
½ teaspoon sea salt
½ teaspoon garlic powder

¼ teaspoon freshly ground black pepper
60 g goat cheese, crumbled
235 ml baby spinach, chopped

Place the steak in a large zip-top bag or between two pieces of plastic wrap. Using a meat mallet or heavy-bottomed skillet, pound the steak to an even ¼-inch thickness. Brush both sides of the steak with the avocado oil. Mix the salt, garlic powder, and pepper in a small dish. Sprinkle this mixture over both sides of the steak. Sprinkle the goat cheese over top, and top that with the spinach. Starting at one of the long sides, roll the steak up tightly. Tie the rolled steak with kitchen string at 3-inch intervals. Set the air fryer to 204ºC. Place the steak roll-up in the air fryer basket. Air fry for 7 minutes. Flip the steak and cook for an additional 7 minutes, until an instant-read thermometer reads 49ºC for medium-rare (adjust the cooking time for your desired doneness).

Beefy Poppers

Prep time: 15 minutes | Cook time: 15 minutes | Makes 8 poppers

8 medium jalapeño peppers, stemmed, halved, and seeded
1 (230 g) package cream cheese (or cream cheese style spread for dairy-free), softened
900 g beef mince (85% lean)

1 teaspoon fine sea salt
½ teaspoon ground black pepper
8 slices thin-cut bacon
Fresh coriander leaves, for garnish

Spray the air fryer basket with avocado oil. Preheat the air fryer to 204ºC. Stuff each jalapeño half with a few tablespoons of cream cheese. Place the halves back together again to form 8 jalapeños. Season the beef mince with the salt and pepper and mix with your hands to incorporate. Flatten about 110 g of beef in the palm of your hand and place a stuffed jalapeño in the center. Fold the beef around the jalapeño, forming an egg shape. Wrap the beef-covered jalapeño with a slice of bacon and secure it with a toothpick. Place the jalapeños in the air fryer basket, leaving space between them (if you're using a smaller air fryer, work in batches if necessary), and air fry for 15 minutes, or until the beef is cooked through and the bacon is crispy. Garnish with coriander before serving. Store leftovers in an airtight container in the fridge for 3 days or in the freezer for up to a month. Reheat in a preheated 176ºC air fryer for 4 minutes, or until heated through and the bacon is crispy.

Ritzy Skirt Steak Fajitas

Prep time: 15 minutes | Cook time: 30 minutes | Serves 4

2 tablespoons olive oil
60 ml lime juice
1 clove garlic, minced
½ teaspoon ground cumin
½ teaspoon hot sauce
½ teaspoon salt
2 tablespoons chopped fresh coriander
450 g skirt steak
1 onion, sliced
1 teaspoon chili powder
1 red pepper, sliced
1 green pepper, sliced
Salt and freshly ground black pepper, to taste
8 flour tortillas
Toppings:
Shredded lettuce
Crumbled feta or ricotta (or grated Cheddar cheese)
Sliced black olives
Diced tomatoes
Sour cream
Guacamole

Combine the olive oil, lime juice, garlic, cumin, hot sauce, salt and coriander in a shallow dish. Add the skirt steak and turn it over several times to coat all sides. Pierce the steak with a needle-style meat tenderizer or paring knife. Marinate the steak in the refrigerator for at least 3 hours, or overnight. When you are ready to cook, remove the steak from the refrigerator and let it sit at room temperature for 30 minutes. Preheat the air fryer to 204ºC. Toss the onion slices with the chili powder and a little olive oil and transfer them to the air fryer basket. Air fry for 5 minutes. Add the red and green peppers to the air fryer basket with the onions, season with salt and pepper and air fry for 8 more minutes, until the onions and peppers are soft. Transfer the vegetables to a dish and cover with aluminum foil to keep warm. Put the skirt steak in the air fryer basket and pour the marinade over the top. Air fry at 204ºC for 12 minutes. Flip the steak over and air fry for an additional 5 minutes. Transfer the cooked steak to a cutting board and let the steak rest for a few minutes. If the peppers and onions need to be heated, return them to the air fryer for just 1 to 2 minutes. Thinly slice the steak at an angle, cutting against the grain of the steak. Serve the steak with the onions and peppers, the warm tortillas and the fajita toppings on the side.

Garlic Butter Steak Bites

Prep time: 5 minutes | Cook time: 16 minutes | Serves 3

Oil, for spraying
450 g boneless steak, cut into 1-inch pieces
2 tablespoons olive oil
1 teaspoon Worcestershire sauce
½ teaspoon granulated garlic
½ teaspoon salt
¼ teaspoon freshly ground black pepper

Preheat the air fryer to 204ºC. Line the air fryer basket with parchment and spray lightly with oil. In a medium bowl, combine the steak, olive oil, Worcestershire sauce, garlic, salt, and black pepper and toss until evenly coated. Place the steak in a single layer in the prepared basket. You may have to work in batches, depending on the size of your air fryer. Cook for 10 to 16 minutes, flipping every 3 to 4 minutes. The total cooking time will depend on the thickness of the meat and your preferred doneness. If you want it well done, it may take up to 5 additional minutes.

Tuscan Air Fried Veal Loin

Prep time: 1 hour 10 minutes | Cook time: 12 minutes | Makes 3 veal chops

1½ teaspoons crushed fennel seeds
1 tablespoon minced fresh rosemary leaves
1 tablespoon minced garlic
1½ teaspoons lemon zest
1½ teaspoons salt
½ teaspoon red pepper flakes
2 tablespoons olive oil
3 (280 g) bone-in veal loin, about ½ inch thick

Combine all the ingredients, except for the veal loin, in a large bowl. Stir to mix well. Dunk the loin in the mixture and press to submerge. Wrap the bowl in plastic and refrigerate for at least an hour to marinate. Preheat the air fryer to 204ºC. Arrange the veal loin in the preheated air fryer and air fry for 12 minutes for medium-rare, or until it reaches your desired doneness. Serve immediately.

Mexican-Style Shredded Beef

Prep time: 5 minutes | Cook time: 35 minutes | Serves 6

1 (900 g) beef braising steak, cut into 2-inch cubes
1 teaspoon salt
½ teaspoon ground black pepper
120 ml no-sugar-added chipotle sauce

In a large bowl, sprinkle beef cubes with salt and pepper and toss to coat. Place beef into ungreased air fryer basket. Adjust the temperature to 204ºC and air fry for 30 minutes, shaking the basket halfway through cooking. Beef will be done when internal temperature is at least 72ºC. Place cooked beef into a large bowl and shred with two forks. Pour in chipotle sauce and toss to coat. Return beef to air fryer basket for an additional 5 minutes at 204ºC to crisp with sauce. Serve warm.

Cheddar Bacon Burst with Spinach

Prep time: 5 minutes | Cook time: 60 minutes | Serves 8

30 slices bacon
1 tablespoon Chipotle chilli powder
2 teaspoons Italian seasoning
120 ml Cheddar cheese
1 L raw spinach

Preheat the air fryer to 192ºC. Weave the bacon into 15 vertical pieces and 12 horizontal pieces. Cut the extra 3 in half to fill in the rest, horizontally. Season the bacon with Chipotle chilli powder and Italian seasoning. Add the cheese to the bacon. Add the spinach and press down to compress. Tightly roll up the woven bacon. Line a baking sheet with kitchen foil and add plenty of salt to it. Put the bacon on top of a cooling rack and put that on top of the baking sheet. Bake for 60 minutes. 1Let cool for 15 minutes before slicing and serving.

Pork Loin with Aloha Salsa

Prep time: 20 minutes | Cook time: 7 to 9 minutes | Serves 4

Aloha Salsa:
235 ml fresh pineapple, chopped in small pieces
60 ml red onion, finely chopped
60 ml green or red pepper, chopped
½ teaspoon ground cinnamon
1 teaspoon reduced-salt soy sauce
⅛ teaspoon crushed red pepper
⅛ teaspoon ground black pepper

2 eggs
2 tablespoons milk
60 ml flour
60 ml panko bread crumbs
4 teaspoons sesame seeds
450 g boneless, thin pork loin or tenderloin (⅜- to ½-inch thick)
Pepper and salt
60 ml cornflour
Oil for misting or cooking spray

In a medium bowl, stir together all ingredients for salsa. Cover and refrigerate while cooking pork. Preheat the air fryer to 200°C. Beat together eggs and milk in shallow dish. In another shallow dish, mix together the flour, panko, and sesame seeds. Sprinkle pork with pepper and salt to taste. Dip pork in cornflour, egg mixture, and then panko coating. Spray both sides with oil or cooking spray. Cook pork for 3 minutes. Turn pork over, spraying both sides, and continue cooking for 4 to 6 minutes or until well done. Serve fried cutlets with salsa on the side.

Almond and Caraway Crust Steak

Prep time: 16 minutes | Cook time: 10 minutes | Serves 4

80 ml almond flour
2 eggs
2 teaspoons caraway seeds
4 beef steaks

2 teaspoons garlic powder
1 tablespoon melted butter
Fine sea salt and cayenne pepper, to taste

Generously coat steaks with garlic powder, caraway seeds, salt, and cayenne pepper. In a mixing dish, thoroughly combine melted butter with seasoned crumbs. In another bowl, beat the eggs until they're well whisked. First, coat steaks with the beaten egg; then, coat beef steaks with the buttered crumb mixture. Place the steaks in the air fryer basket; cook for 10 minutes at 179°C. Bon appétit!

Five-Spice Pork Belly

Prep time: 10 minutes | Cook time: 17 minutes | Serves 4

450 g unsalted pork belly
2 teaspoons Chinese five-spice powder
Sauce:
1 tablespoon coconut oil
1 (1-inch) piece fresh ginger, peeled and grated

2 cloves garlic, minced
120 ml beef or chicken stock
¼ to 120 ml liquid or powdered sweetener
3 tablespoons wheat-free tamari
1 spring onion, sliced, plus more for garnish

Spray the air fryer basket with avocado oil. Preheat the air fryer to 204°C. Cut the pork belly into ½-inch-thick slices and season well on all sides with the five-spice powder. Place the slices in a single layer in the air fryer basket (if you're using a smaller air fryer, work in batches if necessary) and cook for 8 minutes, or until cooked to your liking, flipping halfway through. While the pork belly cooks, make the sauce: Heat the coconut oil in a small saucepan over medium heat. Add the ginger and garlic and sauté for 1 minute, or until fragrant. Add the stock, sweetener, and tamari and simmer for 10 to 15 minutes, until thickened. Add the spring onion and cook for another minute, until the spring onion is softened. Taste and adjust the seasoning to your liking. Transfer the pork belly to a large bowl. Pour the sauce over the pork belly and coat well. Place the pork belly slices on a serving platter and garnish with sliced spring onions. Best served fresh. Store leftovers in an airtight container in the fridge for up to 4 days. Reheat in a preheated 204°C air fryer for 3 minutes, or until heated through.

Sausage and Peppers

Prep time: 7 minutes | Cook time: 35 minutes | Serves 4

Oil, for spraying
900 g hot or sweet Italian-seasoned sausage links, cut into thick slices
4 large peppers of any color, seeded and cut into slices
1 onion, thinly sliced

1 tablespoon olive oil
1 tablespoon chopped fresh parsley
1 teaspoon dried oregano
1 teaspoon dried basil
1 teaspoon balsamic vinegar

Line the air fryer basket with parchment and spray lightly with oil. In a large bowl, combine the sausage, peppers, and onion. In a small bowl, whisk together the olive oil, parsley, oregano, basil, and balsamic vinegar. Pour the mixture over the sausage and peppers and toss until evenly coated. Using a slotted spoon, transfer the mixture to the prepared basket, taking care to drain out as much excess liquid as possible. Air fry at 176°C for 20 minutes, stir, and cook for another 15 minutes, or until the sausage is browned and the juices run clear.

Filipino Crispy Pork Belly

Prep time: 20 minutes | Cook time: 30 minutes | Serves 4

450 g pork belly
700 ml water
6 garlic cloves
2 tablespoons soy sauce

1 teaspoon coarse or flaky salt
1 teaspoon black pepper
2 bay leaves

Cut the pork belly into three thick chunks so it will cook more evenly. Place the pork, water, garlic, soy sauce, salt, pepper, and bay leaves in the inner pot of an Instant Pot or other electric pressure cooker. Seal and cook at high pressure for 15 minutes. Let the pressure release naturally for 10 minutes, then manually release the remaining pressure. (If you do not have a pressure cooker, place all the ingredients in a large saucepan. Cover and cook over low heat until a knife can be easily inserted into the skin side of pork belly, about 1 hour.) Using tongs, very carefully transfer the meat to a wire rack over a rimmed baking sheet to drain and dry for 10 minutes. Cut each chunk of pork belly into two long slices. Arrange the slices in the air fryer basket. Set the air fryer to 204°C for 15 minutes, or until the fat has crisped. Serve immediately.

Sirloin Steak with Honey-Mustard Butter

Prep time: 5 minutes | Cook time: 14 minutes | Serves 4

900 g beef sirloin steak
1 teaspoon cayenne pepper
1 tablespoon honey
1 tablespoon Dijon mustard
½ stick butter, softened
Sea salt and freshly ground black pepper, to taste
Cooking spray

Preheat the air fryer to 204ºC and spritz with cooking spray. Sprinkle the steak with cayenne pepper, salt, and black pepper on a clean work surface. Arrange the steak in the preheated air fryer and spritz with cooking spray. Air fry for 14 minutes or until browned and reach your desired doneness. Flip the steak halfway through. Meanwhile, combine the honey, mustard, and butter in a small bowl. Stir to mix well. Transfer the air fried steak onto a plate and baste with the honey-mustard butter before serving.

Pork Bulgogi

Prep time: 30 minutes | Cook time: 15 minutes | Serves 4

1 onion, thinly sliced
2 tablespoons gochujang (Korean red chili paste)
1 tablespoon minced fresh ginger
1 tablespoon minced garlic
1 tablespoon soy sauce
1 tablespoon Shaoxing wine (rice cooking wine)
1 tablespoon toasted sesame oil
1 teaspoon sugar
¼ to 1 teaspoon cayenne pepper or gochugaru (Korean ground red pepper)
450 g boneless pork shoulder, cut into ½-inch-thick slices
1 tablespoon sesame seeds
60 ml sliced spring onionspring onions

In a large bowl, combine the onion, gochujang, ginger, garlic, soy sauce, wine, sesame oil, sugar, and cayenne. Add the pork and toss to coat. Marinate at room temperature for 30 minutes, or cover and refrigerate for up to 24 hours. Arrange the pork and onion slices in the air fryer basket; discard the marinade. Set the air fryer to 204ºC for 15 minutes, turning the pork halfway through the cooking time. Arrange the pork on a serving platter. Sprinkle with the sesame seeds and spring onionspring onions and serve.

Spicy Rump Steak

Prep time: 25 minutes | Cook time: 12 to 18 minutes | Serves 4

2 tablespoons salsa
1 tablespoon minced chipotle pepper or chipotle paste
1 tablespoon apple cider vinegar
1 teaspoon ground cumin
⅛ teaspoon freshly ground black
pepper
⅛ teaspoon red pepper flakes
340 g rump steak, cut into 4 pieces and gently pounded to about ⅓ inch thick
Cooking oil spray

In a small bowl, thoroughly mix the salsa, chipotle pepper, vinegar, cumin, black pepper, and red pepper flakes. Rub this mixture into both sides of each steak piece. Let stand for 15 minutes at room temperature. Insert the crisper plate into the basket and place the basket into the unit. Preheat the unit by selecting AIR FRY, setting the temperature to 200ºC, and setting the time to 3 minutes. Select START/STOP to begin. Once the unit is preheated, spray the crisper plate with cooking oil. Working in batches, place 2 steaks into the basket. Select AIR FRY, set the temperature to 200ºC, and set the time to 9 minutes. Select START/STOP to begin. After about 6 minutes, check the steaks. If a food thermometer inserted into the meat registers at least 64ºC, they are done. If not, resume cooking. When the cooking is done, transfer the steaks to a clean plate and cover with aluminum foil to keep warm. Repeat steps 3, 4, and 5 with the remaining steaks. Thinly slice the steaks against the grain and serve.

Bone-in Pork Chops

Prep time: 5 minutes | Cook time: 10 to 12 minutes | Serves 2

450 g bone-in pork chops
1 tablespoon avocado oil
1 teaspoon smoked paprika
½ teaspoon onion granules
¼ teaspoon cayenne pepper
Sea salt and freshly ground black pepper, to taste

Brush the pork chops with the avocado oil. In a small dish, mix together the smoked paprika, onion granules, cayenne pepper, and salt and black pepper to taste. Sprinkle the seasonings over both sides of the pork chops. Set the air fryer to 204ºC. Place the chops in the air fryer basket in a single layer, working in batches if necessary. Air fry for 10 to 12 minutes, until an instant-read thermometer reads 64ºC at the chops' thickest point. Remove the chops from the air fryer and allow them to rest for 5 minutes before serving.

Pork and Beef Egg Rolls

Prep time: 30 minutes | Cook time: 7 to 8 minutes per batch | Makes 8 egg rolls

110 g very lean beef mince
110 g lean pork mince
1 tablespoon soy sauce
1 teaspoon olive oil
120 ml grated carrots
2 green onions, chopped
475 ml grated Chinese cabbage
60 ml chopped water chestnuts
¼ teaspoon salt
¼ teaspoon garlic powder
¼ teaspoon black pepper
1 egg
1 tablespoon water
8 egg roll wrappers
Oil for misting or cooking spray

In a large skillet, brown beef and pork with soy sauce. Remove cooked meat from skillet, drain, and set aside. Pour off any excess grease from skillet. Add olive oil, carrots, and onions. Sauté until barely tender, about 1 minute. Stir in cabbage, cover, and cook for 1 minute or just until cabbage slightly wilts. Remove from heat. In a large bowl, combine the cooked meats and vegetables, water chestnuts, salt, garlic powder, and pepper. Stir well. If needed, add more salt to taste. Beat together egg and water in a small bowl. Fill egg roll wrappers, using about 60 ml of filling for each wrap. Roll up and brush all over with egg wash to seal. Spray very lightly with olive oil or cooking spray. Place 4 egg rolls in air fryer basket and air fry at 200ºC for 4 minutes. Turn over and cook 3 to 4 more minutes, until golden brown and crispy. Repeat to cook remaining egg rolls.

Rack of Lamb with Pistachio Crust

Prep time: 10 minutes | Cook time: 19 minutes | Serves 2

120 ml finely chopped pistachios
3 tablespoons panko bread crumbs
1 teaspoon chopped fresh rosemary
2 teaspoons chopped fresh

oregano
Salt and freshly ground black pepper, to taste
1 tablespoon olive oil
1 rack of lamb, bones trimmed of fat and frenched
1 tablespoon Dijon mustard

Preheat the air fryer to 192°C. Combine the pistachios, bread crumbs, rosemary, oregano, salt and pepper in a small bowl. (This is a good job for your food processor if you have one.) Drizzle in the olive oil and stir to combine. Season the rack of lamb with salt and pepper on all sides and transfer it to the air fryer basket with the fat side facing up. Air fry the lamb for 12 minutes. Remove the lamb from the air fryer and brush the fat side of the lamb rack with the Dijon mustard. Coat the rack with the pistachio mixture, pressing the bread crumbs onto the lamb with your hands and rolling the bottom of the rack in any of the crumbs that fall off. Return the rack of lamb to the air fryer and air fry for another 3 to 7 minutes or until an instant read thermometer reads 60°C for medium. Add or subtract a couple of minutes for lamb that is more or less well cooked. (Your time will vary depending on how big the rack of lamb is.) Let the lamb rest for at least 5 minutes. Then, slice into chops and serve.

Savory Sausage Cobbler

Prep time: 15 minutes | Cook time: 34 minutes | Serves 4

Filling:
450 g Italian-seasoned sausage meat, removed from casing
235 ml sliced mushrooms
1 teaspoon fine sea salt
475 ml marinara sauce
Biscuits:
3 large egg whites

180 ml blanched almond flour
1 teaspoon baking powder
¼ teaspoon fine sea salt
2½ tablespoons very cold unsalted butter, cut into ¼-inch pieces
Fresh basil leaves, for garnish

Preheat the air fryer to 204°C. Place the sausage in a pie pan (or a pan that fits into your air fryer). Use your hands to break up the sausage and spread it evenly on the bottom of the pan. Place the pan in the air fryer and air fry for 5 minutes. Remove the pan from the air fryer and use a fork or metal spatula to crumble the sausage more. Season the mushrooms with the salt and add them to the pie pan. Stir to combine the mushrooms and sausage, then return the pan to the air fryer and air fry for 4 minutes, or until the mushrooms are soft and the sausage is cooked through. Remove the pan from the air fryer. Add the marinara sauce and stir well. Set aside. Make the biscuits: Place the egg whites in a large mixing bowl or the bowl of a stand mixer. Using a hand mixer or stand mixer, whip the egg whites until stiff peaks form. In a medium-sized bowl, whisk together the almond flour, baking powder, and salt, then cut in the butter. Gently fold the flour mixture into the egg whites with a rubber spatula. Using a large spoon or ice cream scoop, spoon one-quarter of the dough on top of the sausage mixture, making sure the

butter stays in separate clumps. Repeat with the remaining dough, spacing the biscuits about 1 inch apart. Place the pan in the air fryer and cook for 5 minutes, then lower the heat to 164°C and bake for another 15 to 20 minutes, until the biscuits are golden brown. Serve garnished with fresh basil leaves. Store leftovers in an airtight container in the refrigerator for up to 3 days. Reheat in a preheated 176°C air fryer for 5 minutes, or until warmed through.

Fillet with Crispy Shallots

Prep time: 30 minutes | Cook time: 18 to 20 minutes | Serves 6

680 g beef fillet steaks
Sea salt and freshly ground black pepper, to taste

4 medium shallots
1 teaspoon olive oil or avocado oil

Season both sides of the steaks with salt and pepper, and let them sit at room temperature for 45 minutes. Set the air fryer to 204°C and let it preheat for 5 minutes. Working in batches if necessary, place the steaks in the air fryer basket in a single layer and air fry for 5 minutes. Flip and cook for 5 minutes longer, until an instant-read thermometer inserted in the center of the steaks registers 49°C for medium-rare (or as desired). Remove the steaks and tent with aluminum foil to rest. Set the air fryer to 149°C. In a medium bowl, toss the shallots with the oil. Place the shallots in the basket and air fry for 5 minutes, then give them a toss and cook for 3 to 5 minutes more, until crispy and golden brown. Place the steaks on serving plates and arrange the shallots on top.

Panko Pork Chops

Prep time: 10 minutes | Cook time: 12 minutes | Serves 4

4 boneless pork chops, excess fat trimmed
¼ teaspoon salt
2 eggs
355 ml panko bread crumbs
3 tablespoons grated Parmesan cheese

1½ teaspoons paprika
½ teaspoon granulated garlic
½ teaspoon onion granules
1 teaspoon chili powder
¼ teaspoon freshly ground black pepper
Olive oil spray

Sprinkle the pork chops with salt on both sides and let them sit while you prepare the seasonings and egg wash. In a shallow medium bowl, beat the eggs. In another shallow medium bowl, stir together the panko, Parmesan cheese, paprika, granulated garlic, onion granules, chili powder, and pepper. Dip the pork chops in the egg and in the panko mixture to coat. Firmly press the crumbs onto the chops. Insert the crisper plate into the basket and the basket into the unit. Preheat the unit by selecting AIR ROAST, setting the temperature to 204°C, and setting the time to 3 minutes. Select START/STOP to begin. Once the unit is preheated, spray the crisper plate with olive oil. Place the pork chops into the basket and spray them with olive oil. Select AIR ROAST, set the temperature to 204°C, and set the time to 12 minutes. Select START/STOP to begin. After 6 minutes, flip the pork chops and spray them with more olive oil. Resume cooking. When the cooking is complete, the chops should be golden and crispy and a food thermometer should register 64°C. Serve immediately.

Sausage and Cauliflower Arancini

Prep time: 30 minutes | Cook time: 28 to 32 minutes | Serves 6

Avocado oil spray
170 g Italian-seasoned sausage, casings removed
60 ml diced onion
1 teaspoon minced garlic
1 teaspoon dried thyme
Sea salt and freshly ground black pepper, to taste
120 ml cauliflower rice
85 g cream cheese
110 g Cheddar cheese, shredded
1 large egg
120 ml finely ground blanched almond flour
60 ml finely grated Parmesan cheese
Keto-friendly marinara sauce, for serving

Spray a large skillet with oil and place it over medium-high heat. Once the skillet is hot, put the sausage in the skillet and cook for 7 minutes, breaking up the meat with the back of a spoon. Reduce the heat to medium and add the onion. Cook for 5 minutes, then add the garlic, thyme, and salt and pepper to taste. Cook for 1 minute more. Add the cauliflower rice and cream cheese to the skillet. Cook for 7 minutes, stirring frequently, until the cream cheese melts and the cauliflower is tender. Remove the skillet from the heat and stir in the Cheddar cheese. Using a cookie scoop, form the mixture into 1½-inch balls. Place the balls on a parchment paper-lined baking sheet. Freeze for 30 minutes. Place the egg in a shallow bowl and beat it with a fork. In a separate bowl, stir together the almond flour and Parmesan cheese. Dip the cauliflower balls into the egg, then coat them with the almond flour mixture, gently pressing the mixture to the balls to adhere. Set the air fryer to 204ºC. Spray the cauliflower rice balls with oil, and arrange them in a single layer in the air fryer basket, working in batches if necessary. Air fry for 5 minutes. Flip the rice balls and spray them with more oil. Air fry for 3 to 7 minutes longer, until the balls are golden brown. Serve warm with marinara sauce.

Cheesy Low-Carb Lasagna

Prep time: 10 minutes | Cook time: 10 minutes | Serves 4

Meat Layer:
Extra-virgin olive oil
450 g 85% lean beef mince
235 ml marinara sauce
60 ml diced celery
60 ml diced red onion
½ teaspoon minced garlic
Coarse or flaky salt and black pepper, to taste
Cheese Layer:
230 g ricotta cheese
235 ml shredded Mozzarella cheese
120 ml grated Parmesan cheese
2 large eggs
1 teaspoon dried Italian seasoning, crushed
½ teaspoon each minced garlic, garlic powder, and black pepper

For the meat layer: Grease a cake pan with 1 teaspoon olive oil. In a large bowl, combine the beef mince, marinara, celery, onion, garlic, salt, and pepper. Place the seasoned meat in the pan. Place the pan in the air fryer basket. Set the air fryer to 192ºC for 10 minutes. Meanwhile, for the cheese layer: In a medium bowl, combine the ricotta, half the Mozzarella, the Parmesan, lightly beaten eggs, Italian seasoning, minced garlic, garlic powder, and pepper. Stir until well blended. At the end of the cooking time, spread the cheese mixture over the meat mixture. Sprinkle with the remaining

120 ml Mozzarella. Set the air fryer to 192ºC for 10 minutes, or until the cheese is browned and bubbling. At the end of the cooking time, use a meat thermometer to ensure the meat has reached an internal temperature of 72ºC. Drain the fat and liquid from the pan. Let stand for 5 minutes before serving.

Spice-Rubbed Pork Loin

Prep time: 5 minutes | Cook time: 20 minutes | Serves 6

1 teaspoon paprika
½ teaspoon ground cumin
½ teaspoon chili powder
½ teaspoon garlic powder
2 tablespoons coconut oil
1 (680 g) boneless pork loin
½ teaspoon salt
¼ teaspoon ground black pepper

In a small bowl, mix paprika, cumin, chili powder, and garlic powder. Drizzle coconut oil over pork. Sprinkle pork loin with salt and pepper, then rub spice mixture evenly on all sides. Place pork loin into ungreased air fryer basket. Adjust the temperature to 204ºC and air fry for 20 minutes, turning pork halfway through cooking. Pork loin will be browned and have an internal temperature of at least 64ºC when done. Serve warm.

Parmesan Herb Filet Mignon

Prep time: 20 minutes | Cook time: 13 minutes | Serves 4

450 g filet mignon
Sea salt and ground black pepper, to taste
½ teaspoon cayenne pepper
1 teaspoon dried basil
1 teaspoon dried rosemary
1 teaspoon dried thyme
1 tablespoon sesame oil
1 small-sized egg, well-whisked
120 ml Parmesan cheese, grated

Season the filet mignon with salt, black pepper, cayenne pepper, basil, rosemary, and thyme. Brush with sesame oil. Put the egg in a shallow plate. Now, place the Parmesan cheese in another plate. Coat the filet mignon with the egg; then lay it into the Parmesan cheese. Set the air fryer to 182ºC. Cook for 10 to 13 minutes or until golden. Serve with mixed salad leaves and enjoy!

Mexican Pork Chops

Prep time: 5 minutes | Cook time: 15 minutes | Serves 2

¼ teaspoon dried oregano
1½ teaspoons taco seasoning or fajita seasoning mix
2 (110 g) boneless pork chops
2 tablespoons unsalted butter, divided

Preheat the air fryer to 204ºC. Combine the dried oregano and taco seasoning in a small bowl and rub the mixture into the pork chops. Brush the chops with 1 tablespoon butter. In the air fryer, air fry the chops for 15 minutes, turning them over halfway through to air fry on the other side. When the chops are a brown color, check the internal temperature has reached 64ºC and remove from the air fryer. Serve with a garnish of remaining butter.

Lamb Chops with Horseradish Sauce

Prep time: 30 minutes | Cook time: 13 minutes | Serves 4

Lamb:
4 lamb loin chops
2 tablespoons vegetable oil
1 clove garlic, minced
½ teaspoon coarse or flaky salt
½ teaspoon black pepper

Horseradish Cream Sauce:
120 ml mayonnaise
1 tablespoon Dijon mustard
1 to 1½ tablespoons grated horseradish
2 teaspoons sugar
Vegetable oil spray

For the lamb: Brush the lamb chops with the oil, rub with the garlic, and sprinkle with the salt and pepper. Marinate at room temperature for 30 minutes. Meanwhile, for the sauce: In a medium bowl, combine the mayonnaise, mustard, horseradish, and sugar. Stir until well combined. Set aside half of the sauce for serving. Spray the air fryer basket with vegetable oil spray and place the chops in the basket. Set the air fryer to 164°C for 10 minutes, turning the chops halfway through the cooking time. Remove the chops from the air fryer and add to the bowl with the horseradish sauce, turning to coat with the sauce. Place the chops back in the air fryer basket. Set the air fryer to 204°C for 3 minutes. Use a meat thermometer to ensure the meat has reached an internal temperature of 64°C (for medium-rare). Serve the chops with the reserved horseradish sauce.

Beef and Tomato Sauce Meatloaf

Prep time: 15 minutes | Cook time: 25 minutes | Serves 4

680 g beef mince
235 ml tomato sauce
120 ml breadcrumbs
2 egg whites
120 ml grated Parmesan cheese
1 diced onion
2 tablespoons chopped parsley

2 tablespoons minced ginger
2 garlic cloves, minced
½ teaspoon dried basil
1 teaspoon cayenne pepper
Salt and ground black pepper, to taste
Cooking spray

Preheat the air fryer to 182°C. Spritz a meatloaf pan with cooking spray. Combine all the ingredients in a large bowl. Stir to mix well. Pour the meat mixture in the prepared meatloaf pan and press with a spatula to make it firm. Arrange the pan in the preheated air fryer and bake for 25 minutes or until the beef is well browned. Serve immediately.

Chapter 8 Fish and Seafood

Chapter 8 Fish and Seafood

Catfish Bites

Prep time: 15 minutes | Cook time: 20 minutes | Serves 4

Olive or vegetable oil, for spraying
455 g catfish fillets, cut into 2-inch pieces
235 ml buttermilk
70 g cornmeal
30 g plain flour
2 teaspoons Creole seasoning
120 ml yellow mustard

Line the air fryer basket with baking paper and spray lightly with oil. Place the catfish pieces and buttermilk in a zip-top plastic bag, seal, and refrigerate for about 10 minutes. In a shallow bowl, mix together the cornmeal, flour, and Creole seasoning. Remove the catfish from the bag and pat dry with a paper towel. Spread the mustard on all sides of the catfish, then dip them in the cornmeal mixture until evenly coated. Place the catfish in the prepared basket. You may need to work in batches, depending on the size of your air fryer. Spray lightly with oil. Air fry at 204°C for 10 minutes, flip carefully, spray with oil, and cook for another 10 minutes. Serve immediately.

Tuna Avocado Bites

Prep time: 10 minutes | Cook time: 7 minutes | Makes 12 bites

280 g can tuna, drained
60 ml full-fat mayonnaise
1 stalk celery, chopped
1 medium avocado, peeled,
pitted, and mashed
50 g blanched finely ground almond flour, divided
2 teaspoons coconut oil

In a large bowl, mix tuna, mayonnaise, celery, and mashed avocado. Form the mixture into balls. Roll balls in almond flour and spritz with coconut oil. Place balls into the air fryer basket. Adjust the temperature to 204°C and set the timer for 7 minutes. Gently turn tuna bites after 5 minutes. Serve warm.

Roasted Halibut Steaks with Parsley

Prep time: 5 minutes | Cook time: 10 minutes | Serves 4

455 g halibut steaks
60 ml vegetable oil
2½ tablespoons Worcester sauce
2 tablespoons honey
2 tablespoons vermouth or white wine vinegar
1 tablespoon freshly squeezed lemon juice
1 tablespoon fresh parsley leaves, coarsely chopped
Salt and pepper, to taste
1 teaspoon dried basil

Preheat the air fryer to 200°C. Put all the ingredients in a large mixing dish and gently stir until the fish is coated evenly. Transfer the fish to the air fryer basket and roast for 10 minutes, flipping the fish halfway through, or until the fish reaches an internal temperature of at least 64°C on a meat thermometer. Let the fish cool for 5 minutes and serve.

Cayenne Sole Cutlets

Prep time: 15 minutes | Cook time: 10 minutes | Serves 2

1 egg
120 g Pecorino Romano cheese, grated
Sea salt and white pepper, to
taste
½ teaspoon cayenne pepper
1 teaspoon dried parsley flakes
2 sole fillets

To make a breading station, whisk the egg until frothy. In another bowl, mix Pecorino Romano cheese, and spices. Dip the fish in the egg mixture and turn to coat evenly; then, dredge in the cracker crumb mixture, turning a couple of times to coat evenly. Cook in the preheated air fryer at 200°C for 5 minutes; turn them over and cook another 5 minutes. Enjoy!

Seasoned Tuna Steaks

Prep time: 5 minutes | Cook time: 9 minutes | Serves 4

1 teaspoon garlic powder
½ teaspoon salt
¼ teaspoon dried thyme
¼ teaspoon dried oregano
4 tuna steaks
2 tablespoons olive oil
1 lemon, quartered

Preheat the air fryer to 192°C. In a small bowl, whisk together the garlic powder, salt, thyme, and oregano. Coat the tuna steaks with olive oil. Season both sides of each steak with the seasoning blend. Place the steaks in a single layer in the air fryer basket. Roast for 5 minutes, then flip and roast for an additional 3 to 4 minutes.

Bacon Halibut Steak

Prep time: 15 minutes | Cook time: 10 minutes | Serves 4

680 g halibut steaks (170 g each fillet)
1 teaspoon avocado oil
1 teaspoon ground black pepper
110 g bacon, sliced

Sprinkle the halibut steaks with avocado oil and ground black pepper. Then wrap the fish in the bacon slices and put in the air fryer. Cook the fish at 200°C for 5 minutes per side.

Orange-Mustard Glazed Salmon

Prep time: 10 minutes | Cook time: 10 minutes | Serves 2

1 tablespoon orange marmalade	2 (230 g) skin-on salmon fillets,
¼ teaspoon grated orange zest plus 1 tablespoon juice	1½ inches thick
	Salt and pepper, to taste
2 teaspoons whole-grain mustard	Vegetable oil spray

Preheat the air fryer to 204ºC. Make foil sling for air fryer basket by folding 1 long sheet of aluminum foil so it is 4 inches wide. Lay sheet of foil widthwise across basket, pressing foil into and up sides of basket. Fold excess foil as needed so that edges of foil are flush with top of basket. Lightly spray foil and basket with vegetable oil spray. Combine marmalade, orange zest and juice, and mustard in bowl. Pat salmon dry with paper towels and season with salt and pepper. Brush tops and sides of fillets evenly with glaze. Arrange fillets skin side down on sling in prepared basket, spaced evenly apart. Air fry salmon until center is still translucent when checked with the tip of a paring knife and registers 52ºC (for medium-rare), 10 to 14 minutes, using sling to rotate fillets halfway through cooking. Using the sling, carefully remove salmon from air fryer. Slide fish spatula along underside of fillets and transfer to individual serving plates, leaving skin behind. Serve.

Lemon Pepper Prawns

Prep time: 15 minutes | Cook time: 8 minutes | Serves 2

Olive or vegetable oil, for spraying	1 tablespoon olive oil
	1 teaspoon lemon pepper
340 g medium raw prawns, peeled and deveined	¼ teaspoon paprika
	¼ teaspoon granulated garlic
3 tablespoons lemon juice	

Preheat the air fryer to 204ºC. Line the air fryer basket with baking paper and spray lightly with oil. In a medium bowl, toss together the prawns, lemon juice, olive oil, lemon pepper, paprika, and garlic until evenly coated. Place the prawns in the prepared basket. Cook for 6 to 8 minutes, or until pink and firm. Serve immediately.

South Indian Fried Fish

Prep time: 20 minutes | Cook time: 8 minutes | Serves 4

2 tablespoons olive oil	salt
2 tablespoons fresh lime or lemon juice	¼ to ½ teaspoon cayenne pepper
	455 g tilapia fillets (2 to 3
1 teaspoon minced fresh ginger	fillets)
1 clove garlic, minced	Olive oil spray
1 teaspoon ground turmeric	Lime or lemon wedges
½ teaspoon kosher or coarse sea	(optional)

In a large bowl, combine the oil, lime juice, ginger, garlic, turmeric, salt, and cayenne. Stir until well combined; set aside. Cut each tilapia fillet into three or four equal-size pieces. Add the fish to the bowl and gently mix until all of the fish is coated in the marinade. Marinate for 10 to 15 minutes at room temperature. (Don't marinate any longer or the acid in the lime juice will "cook" the fish.) Spray the air fryer basket with olive oil spray. Place the fish in the basket and spray the fish. Set the air fryer to 164ºC for 3 minutes to partially cook the fish. Set the air fryer to 204ºC for 5 minutes to finish cooking and crisp up the fish. (Thinner pieces of fish will cook faster so you may want to check at the 3-minute mark of the second cooking time and remove those that are cooked through, and then add them back toward the end of the second cooking time to crisp.) Carefully remove the fish from the basket. Serve hot, with lemon wedges if desired.

Prawn and Cherry Tomato Kebabs

Prep time: 15 minutes | Cook time: 5 minutes | Serves 4

680 g jumbo prawns, cleaned, peeled and deveined	½ teaspoon dried basil
	½ teaspoon dried oregano
455 g cherry tomatoes	½ teaspoon mustard seeds
2 tablespoons butter, melted	½ teaspoon marjoram
1 tablespoons Sriracha sauce	Special Equipment:
Sea salt and ground black pepper, to taste	4 to 6 wooden skewers, soaked in water for 30 minutes
1 teaspoon dried parsley flakes	

Preheat the air fryer to 204ºC. Put all the ingredients in a large bowl and toss to coat well. Make the kebabs: Thread, alternating jumbo prawns and cherry tomatoes, onto the wooden skewers that fit into the air fryer. Arrange the kebabs in the air fryer basket. You may need to cook in batches depending on the size of your air fryer basket. Air fry for 5 minutes, or until the prawns are pink and the cherry tomatoes are softened. Repeat with the remaining kebabs. Let the prawns and cherry tomato kebabs cool for 5 minutes and serve hot.

Lemony Prawns and Courgette

Prep time: 15 minutes | Cook time: 7 to 8 minutes | Serves 4

570 g extra-large raw prawns, peeled and deveined	1½ teaspoons dried oregano
	⅛ teaspoon crushed red pepper flakes (optional)
2 medium courgettes (about 230 g each), halved lengthwise and cut into ½-inch-thick slices	Juice of ½ lemon
	1 tablespoon chopped fresh mint
1½ tablespoons olive oil	1 tablespoon chopped fresh dill
½ teaspoon garlic salt	

Preheat the air fryer to 176ºC. In a large bowl, combine the prawns, courgette, oil, garlic salt, oregano, and pepper flakes (if using) and toss to coat. Working in batches, arrange a single layer of the prawns and courgette in the air fryer basket. Air fry for 7 to 8 minutes, shaking the basket halfway, until the courgette is golden and the prawns are cooked through. Transfer to a serving dish and tent with foil while you air fry the remaining prawns and courgette. Top with the lemon juice, mint, and dill and serve.

Sweet Tilapia Fillets

Prep time: 5 minutes | Cook time: 14 minutes | Serves 4

2 tablespoons granulated sweetener
1 tablespoon apple cider vinegar

4 tilapia fillets, boneless
1 teaspoon olive oil

Mix apple cider vinegar with olive oil and sweetener. Then rub the tilapia fillets with the sweet mixture and put in the air fryer basket in one layer. Cook the fish at 182°C for 7 minutes per side.

chilli Tilapia

Prep time: 5 minutes | Cook time: 20 minutes | Serves 4

4 tilapia fillets, boneless
1 teaspoon chilli flakes
1 teaspoon dried oregano

1 tablespoon avocado oil
1 teaspoon mustard

Rub the tilapia fillets with chilli flakes, dried oregano, avocado oil, and mustard and put in the air fryer. Cook it for 10 minutes per side at 182°C.

Asian Marinated Salmon

Prep time: 30 minutes | Cook time: 6 minutes | Serves 2

Marinade:
60 ml wheat-free tamari or coconut aminos
2 tablespoons lime or lemon juice
2 tablespoons sesame oil
2 tablespoons powdered sweetener
2 teaspoons grated fresh ginger
2 cloves garlic, minced
½ teaspoon ground black pepper

2 (110 g) salmon fillets (about 1¼ inches thick)
Sliced spring onions, for garnish
Sauce (Optional):
60 ml beef stock
60 ml wheat-free tamari
3 tablespoons powdered sweetener
1 tablespoon tomato sauce
⅛ teaspoon guar gum or xanthan gum (optional, for thickening)

Make the marinade: In a medium-sized shallow dish, stir together all the ingredients for the marinade until well combined. Place the salmon in the marinade. Cover and refrigerate for at least 2 hours or overnight. Preheat the air fryer to 204°C. Remove the salmon fillets from the marinade and place them in the air fryer, leaving space between them. Air fry for 6 minutes, or until the salmon is cooked through and flakes easily with a fork. While the salmon cooks, make the sauce, if using: Place all the sauce ingredients except the guar gum in a medium-sized bowl and stir until well combined. Taste and adjust the sweetness to your liking. While whisking slowly, add the guar gum. Allow the sauce to thicken for 3 to 5 minutes. (The sauce can be made up to 3 days ahead and stored in an airtight container in the fridge.) Drizzle the sauce over the salmon before serving. Garnish the salmon with sliced spring onions before serving. Store leftovers in an airtight container in the fridge for up to 3 days. Reheat in a preheated 176°C air fryer for 3 minutes, or until heated through.

Crispy Fish Sticks

Prep time: 15 minutes | Cook time: 10 minutes | Serves 4

30 g crushed panko breadcrumbs
25 g blanched finely ground almond flour
½ teaspoon Old Bay seasoning

1 tablespoon coconut oil
1 large egg
455 g cod fillet, cut into ¾-inch strips

Place panko, almond flour, Old Bay seasoning, and coconut oil into a large bowl and mix together. In a medium bowl, whisk egg. Dip each fish stick into the egg and then gently press into the flour mixture, coating as fully and evenly as possible. Place fish sticks into the air fryer basket. Adjust the temperature to 204°C and air fry for 10 minutes or until golden. Serve immediately.

Crab Cakes with Bell Peppers

Prep time: 5 minutes | Cook time: 10 minutes | Serves 4

230 g jumbo lump crab meat
1 egg, beaten
Juice of ½ lemon
50 g bread crumbs
35 g diced green bell pepper

35 g diced red bell pepper
60 g mayonnaise
1 tablespoon Old Bay seasoning
1 teaspoon plain flour
Cooking spray

Preheat the air fryer to 190°C. Make the crab cakes: Place all the ingredients except the flour and oil in a large bowl and stir until well incorporated. Divide the crab mixture into four equal portions and shape each portion into a patty with your hands. Top each patty with a sprinkle of ¼ teaspoon of flour. Arrange the crab cakes in the air fryer basket and spritz them with cooking spray. Air fry for 10 minutes, flipping the crab cakes halfway through, or until they are cooked through. Divide the crab cakes among four plates and serve.

Tuna and Fruit Kebabs

Prep time: 15 minutes | Cook time: 8 to 12 minutes | Serves 4

455 g tuna steaks, cut into 1-inch cubes
85 g canned pineapple chunks, drained, juice reserved
75 g large red grapes

1 tablespoon honey
2 teaspoons grated fresh ginger
1 teaspoon olive oil
Pinch cayenne pepper

Thread the tuna, pineapple, and grapes on 8 bamboo or 4 metal skewers that fit in the air fryer. In a small bowl, whisk the honey, 1 tablespoon of reserved pineapple juice, the ginger, olive oil, and cayenne. Brush this mixture over the kebabs. Let them stand for 10 minutes. Air fry the kebabs at 188°C for 8 to 12 minutes, or until the tuna reaches an internal temperature of at least 64°C on a meat thermometer, and the fruit is tender and glazed, brushing once with the remaining sauce. Discard any remaining marinade. Serve immediately.

Salmon on Bed of Fennel and Carrot

Prep time: 15 minutes | Cook time: 13 to 14 minutes | Serves 2

1 fennel bulb, thinly sliced
1 large carrot, peeled and sliced
1 small onion, thinly sliced
60 ml low-fat sour cream
¼ teaspoon coarsely ground pepper
2 salmon fillets, 140 g each

Combine the fennel, carrot, and onion in a bowl and toss. Put the vegetable mixture into a baking pan. Roast in the air fryer at204ºC for 4 minutes or until the vegetables are crisp-tender. Remove the pan from the air fryer. Stir in the sour cream and sprinkle the vegetables with the pepper. Top with the salmon fillets. Return the pan to the air fryer. Roast for another 9 to 10 minutes or until the salmon just barely flakes when tested with a fork.

Air Fryer Fish Fry

Prep time: 5 minutes | Cook time: 15 minutes | Serves 4

470 ml low-fat buttermilk
½ teaspoon garlic powder
½ teaspoon onion powder
4 (110 g) sole fillets
70 g plain yellow cornmeal
45 g chickpea flour
¼ teaspoon cayenne pepper
Freshly ground black pepper

In a large bowl, combine the buttermilk, garlic powder, and onion powder. Add the sole, turning until well coated, and set aside to marinate for 20 minutes. In a shallow bowl, stir the cornmeal, chickpea flour, cayenne, and pepper together. Dredge the fillets in the meal mixture, turning until well coated. Place in the basket of an air fryer. Set the air fryer to 192ºC, close, and cook for 12 minutes.

Garlic Prawns

Prep time: 15 minutes | Cook time: 10 minutes | Serves 3

Prawns:
Olive or vegetable oil, for spraying
450 g medium raw prawns, peeled and deveined
6 tablespoons unsalted butter, melted
120 g panko bread crumbs
2 tablespoons garlic granules
1 teaspoon salt
½ teaspoon freshly ground black pepper
Garlic Butter Sauce:
115 g unsalted butter
2 teaspoons garlic granules
¾ teaspoon salt (omit if using salted butter)

Make the Prawns Preheat the air fryer to 204ºC. Line the air fryer basket with baking paper and spray lightly with oil. Place the prawns and melted butter in a zip-top plastic bag, seal, and shake well, until evenly coated. In a medium bowl, mix together the breadcrumbs, garlic, salt, and black pepper. Add the prawns to the panko mixture and toss until evenly coated. Shake off any excess coating. Place the prawns in the prepared basket and spray lightly with oil. Cook for 8 to 10 minutes, flipping and spraying with oil after 4 to 5 minutes, until golden brown and crispy. Make the Garlic Butter Sauce In a microwave-safe bowl, combine the butter, garlic, and salt and microwave on 50% power for 30 to 60 seconds, stirring every 15 seconds, until completely melted. Serve the prawns immediately with the garlic butter sauce on the side for dipping.

Country Prawns

Prep time: 10 minutes | Cook time: 15 to 20 minutes | Serves 4

455 g large prawns, peeled and deveined, with tails on
455 g smoked sausage, cut into thick slices
2 corn cobs, quartered
1 courgette, cut into bite-sized
pieces
1 red bell pepper, cut into chunks
1 tablespoon Old Bay seasoning
2 tablespoons olive oil
Cooking spray

Preheat the air fryer to 204ºC. Spray the air fryer basket lightly with cooking spray. In a large bowl, mix the prawns, sausage, corn, courgette, bell pepper, and Old Bay seasoning, and toss to coat with the spices. Add the olive oil and toss again until evenly coated. Spread the mixture in the air fryer basket in a single layer. You will need to cook in batches. Air fry for 15 to 20 minutes, or until cooked through, shaking the basket every 5 minutes for even cooking. Serve immediately.

Stuffed Sole Florentine

Prep time: 10 minutes | Cook time: 25 minutes | Serves 4

40 g pine nuts
2 tablespoons olive oil
90 g chopped tomatoes
170 g bag spinach, coarsely chopped
2 cloves garlic, chopped
Salt and freshly ground black
pepper, to taste
2 tablespoons unsalted butter, divided
4 Sole fillets (about 680 g)
Dash of paprika
½ lemon, sliced into 4 wedges

Place the pine nuts in a baking dish that fits in your air fryer. Set the air fryer to 204ºC and air fry for 4 minutes until the nuts are lightly browned and fragrant. Remove the baking dish from the air fryer, tip the nuts onto a plate to cool, and continue preheating the air fryer. When the nuts are cool enough to handle, chop them into fine pieces. In the baking dish, combine the oil, tomatoes, spinach, and garlic. Use tongs to toss until thoroughly combined. Air fry for 5 minutes until the tomatoes are softened and the spinach is wilted. Transfer the vegetables to a bowl and stir in the toasted pine nuts. Season to taste with salt and freshly ground black pepper. Place 1 tablespoon of the butter in the bottom of the baking dish. Lower the heat on the air fryer to 176ºC. Place the sole on a clean work surface. Sprinkle both sides with salt and black pepper. Divide the vegetable mixture among the sole fillets and carefully roll up, securing with toothpicks. Working in batches if necessary, arrange the fillets seam-side down in the baking dish along with 1 tablespoon of water. Top the fillets with remaining 1 tablespoon butter and sprinkle with a dash of paprika. 7.Cover loosely with foil and air fry for 10 to 15 minutes until the fish is opaque and flakes easily with a fork. Remove the toothpicks before serving with the lemon wedges.

Maple Balsamic Glazed Salmon

Prep time: 5 minutes | Cook time: 10 minutes | Serves 4

4 fillets of salmon, 170 g each
Salt and freshly ground black pepper, to taste
Vegetable oil

60 ml pure maple syrup
3 tablespoons balsamic vinegar
1 teaspoon Dijon mustard

Preheat the air fryer to 204ºC. Season the salmon well with salt and freshly ground black pepper. Spray or brush the bottom of the air fryer basket with vegetable oil and place the salmon fillets inside. Air fry the salmon for 5 minutes. While the salmon is air frying, combine the maple syrup, balsamic vinegar and Dijon mustard in a small saucepan over medium heat and stir to blend well. Let the mixture simmer while the fish is cooking. It should start to thicken slightly, but keep your eye on it so it doesn't burn. Brush the glaze on the salmon fillets and air fry for an additional 5 minutes. The salmon should feel firm to the touch when finished and the glaze should be nicely browned on top. Brush a little more glaze on top before removing and serving with rice and vegetables, or a nice green salad.

Honey-Balsamic Salmon

Prep time: 5 minutes | Cook time: 8 minutes | Serves 2

Olive or vegetable oil, for spraying
2 (170 g) salmon fillets
60 ml balsamic vinegar
2 tablespoons honey

2 teaspoons red pepper flakes
2 teaspoons olive oil
½ teaspoon salt
¼ teaspoon freshly ground black pepper

Line the air fryer basket with baking paper and spray lightly with oil. Place the salmon in the prepared basket. In a small bowl, whisk together the balsamic vinegar, honey, red pepper flakes, olive oil, salt, and black pepper. Brush the mixture over the salmon. Roast at 200ºC for 7 to 8 minutes, or until the internal temperature reaches 64ºC. Serve immediately.

Lemony Prawns

Prep time: 10 minutes | Cook time: 7 to 8 minutes | Serves 4

455 g prawns, peeled and deveined
4 tablespoons olive oil
1½ tablespoons lemon juice
1½ tablespoons fresh parsley, roughly chopped

2 cloves garlic, finely minced
1 teaspoon crushed red pepper flakes, or more to taste
Garlic pepper, to taste
Sea salt flakes, to taste

Preheat the air fryer to 196ºC. Toss all the ingredients in a large bowl until the prawns are coated on all sides. Arrange the prawns in the air fryer basket and air fry for 7 to 8 minutes, or until the prawns are pink and cooked through. Serve warm.

Cod Tacos with Mango Salsa

Prep time: 15 minutes | Cook time: 17 minutes | Serves 4

1 mango, peeled and diced
1 small jalapeño pepper, diced
½ red bell pepper, diced
½ red onion, minced
Pinch chopped fresh cilantro
Juice of ½ lime
¼ teaspoon salt
¼ teaspoon ground black pepper
120 ml Mexican beer

1 egg
75 g cornflour
90 g plain flour
½ teaspoon ground cumin
¼ teaspoon chilli powder
455 g cod, cut into 4 pieces
Olive oil spray
4 corn tortillas, or flour tortillas, at room temperature

In a small bowl, stir together the mango, jalapeño, red bell pepper, red onion, cilantro, lime juice, salt, and pepper. Set aside. In a medium bowl, whisk the beer and egg. In another medium bowl, stir together the cornflour, flour, cumin, and chilli powder. Insert the crisper plate into the basket and the basket into the unit. Preheat the unit to 192ºC. Dip the fish pieces into the egg mixture and in the flour mixture to coat completely. Once the unit is preheated, place a baking paper liner into the basket. Place the fish on the liner in a single layer. Cook for about 9 minutes, spray the fish with olive oil. Reinsert the basket to resume cooking. When the cooking is complete, the fish should be golden and crispy. Place the pieces in the tortillas, top with the mango salsa, and serve.

Bang Bang Prawns

Prep time: 15 minutes | Cook time: 14 minutes | Serves 4

Sauce:
115 g mayonnaise
60 ml sweet chilli sauce
2 to 4 tablespoons Sriracha
1 teaspoon minced fresh ginger
Prawns:
455 g jumbo raw prawns (21 to

25 count), peeled and deveined
2 tablespoons cornflour or rice flour
½ teaspoon kosher or coarse sea salt
Vegetable oil spray

For the sauce: In a large bowl, combine the mayonnaise, chilli sauce, Sriracha, and ginger. Stir until well combined. Remove half of the sauce to serve as a dipping sauce. For the prawns: Place the prawns in a medium bowl. Sprinkle the cornflour and salt over the prawns and toss until well coated. Place the prawns in the air fryer basket in a single layer. (If they won't fit in a single layer, set a rack or trivet on top of the bottom layer of prawns and place the rest of the prawns on the rack.) Spray generously with vegetable oil spray. Set the air fryer to 176ºC for 10 minutes, turning and spraying with additional oil spray halfway through the cooking time. Remove the prawns and toss in the bowl with half of the sauce. Place the prawns back in the air fryer basket. Cook for an additional 4 to 5 minutes, or until the sauce has formed a glaze. Serve the hot prawns with the reserved sauce for dipping.

Black Cod with Grapes and Kale

Prep time: 10 minutes | Cook time: 15 minutes | Serves 2

2 fillets of black cod, 200 g each
Salt and freshly ground black pepper, to taste
Olive oil
150 g grapes, halved
1 small bulb fennel, sliced ¼-inch thick

65 g pecans
200 g shredded kale
2 teaspoons white balsamic vinegar or white wine vinegar
2 tablespoons extra-virgin olive oil

Preheat the air fryer to 204ºC. Season the cod fillets with salt and pepper and drizzle, brush or spray a little olive oil on top. Place the fish, presentation side up (skin side down), into the air fryer basket. Air fry for 10 minutes. When the fish has finished cooking, remove the fillets to a side plate and loosely tent with foil to rest. Toss the grapes, fennel and pecans in a bowl with a drizzle of olive oil and season with salt and pepper. Add the grapes, fennel and pecans to the air fryer basket and air fry for 5 minutes, shaking the basket once during the cooking time. Transfer the grapes, fennel and pecans to a bowl with the kale. Dress the kale with the balsamic vinegar and olive oil, season to taste with salt and pepper and serve alongside the cooked fish.

Lemony Salmon

Prep time: 30 minutes | Cook time: 10 minutes | Serves 4

680 g salmon steak
½ teaspoon grated lemon zest
Freshly cracked mixed peppercorns, to taste
80 ml lemon juice

Fresh chopped chives, for garnish
120 ml dry white wine, or apple cider vinegar
½ teaspoon fresh coriander, chopped
Fine sea salt, to taste

To prepare the marinade, place all ingredients, except for salmon steak and chives, in a deep pan. Bring to a boil over medium-high flame until it has reduced by half. Allow it to cool down. After that, allow salmon steak to marinate in the refrigerator approximately 40 minutes. Discard the marinade and transfer the fish steak to the preheated air fryer. Air fry at 204ºC for 9 to 10 minutes. To finish, brush hot fish steaks with the reserved marinade, garnish with fresh chopped chives, and serve right away!

Snapper with Fruit

Prep time: 15 minutes | Cook time: 9 to 13 minutes | Serves 4

4 red snapper fillets, 100 g each
2 teaspoons olive oil
3 nectarines, halved and pitted
3 plums, halved and pitted

150 g red grapes
1 tablespoon freshly squeezed lemon juice
1 tablespoon honey
½ teaspoon dried thyme

Put the red snapper in the air fryer basket and drizzle with the olive oil. Air fry at 200ºC for 4 minutes. Remove the basket and add the nectarines and plums. Scatter the grapes over all. Drizzle with the lemon juice and honey and sprinkle with the thyme. Return the basket to the air fryer and air fry for 5 to 9 minutes more, or until the fish flakes when tested with a fork and the fruit is tender. Serve immediately.

Chapter 9 Holiday Specials

Chapter 9 Holiday Specials

Classic Latkes

Prep time: 15 minutes | Cook time: 10 minutes | Makes 4 latkes

1 egg
2 tablespoons plain flour
2 medium potatoes, peeled and shredded, rinsed and drained
¼ teaspoon granulated garlic
½ teaspoon salt
Cooking spray

Preheat the air fryer to 192ºC. Spritz the air fryer basket with cooking spray. Whisk together the egg, flour, potatoes, garlic, and salt in a large bowl. Stir to mix well. Divide the mixture into four parts, then flatten them into four circles. Arrange the circles into the preheated air fryer. Spritz the circles with cooking spray, then air fry for 10 minutes or until golden brown and crispy. Flip the latkes halfway through. Serve immediately.

Custard Donut Holes with Chocolate Glaze

Prep time: 1 hour 50 minutes | Cook time: 4 minutes per batch | Makes 24 donut holes

Dough:
350 ml bread flour
2 egg yolks
1 teaspoon active dry yeast
120 ml warm milk
½ teaspoon pure vanilla extract
2 tablespoons butter, melted
1 tablespoon sugar
¼ teaspoon salt
Cooking spray

Custard Filling:
1 (96 g) box French vanilla instant pudding mix
60 ml double cream
180 ml whole milk
Chocolate Glaze:
80 ml double cream
235 ml chocolate chips
Special Equipment:
A pastry bag with a long tip

Combine the ingredients for the dough in a food processor, then pulse until a satiny dough ball forms. Transfer the dough on a lightly floured work surface, then knead for 2 minutes by hand and shape the dough back to a ball. Spritz a large bowl with cooking spray, then transfer the dough ball into the bowl. Wrap the bowl in plastic and let it rise for 1½ hours or until it doubled in size. Transfer the risen dough on a floured work surface, then shape it into a 24-inch-long log. Cut the log into 24 parts and shape each part into a ball. Transfer the balls on two or three baking sheets and let sit to rise for 30 more minutes. Preheat the air fryer to 204ºC. Arrange the baking sheets in the air fryer. You need to work in batches to avoid overcrowding. Spritz the balls with cooking spray. Bake for 4 minutes or until golden brown. Flip the balls halfway through. Meanwhile, combine the ingredients for the filling in a large bowl and whisk for 2 minutes with a hand mixer until well combined. Pour the double cream in a saucepan, then bring to a boil. Put the chocolate chips in a small bowl and pour in the boiled double cream immediately. Mix until the chocolate chips are melted, and the mixture is smooth. Transfer the baked donut holes to a large plate, then pierce a hole into each donut hole and lightly hollow them. Pour the filling in a pastry bag with a long tip and gently squeeze the filling into the donut holes. Then top the donut holes with chocolate glaze. Allow to sit for 10 minutes, then serve.

Simple Butter Cake

Prep time: 25 minutes | Cook time: 20 minutes | Serves 8

235 ml plain flour
1¼ teaspoons baking powder
¼ teaspoon salt
120 ml plus 1½ tablespoons granulated white sugar
9½ tablespoons butter, at room
temperature
2 large eggs
1 large egg yolk
2½ tablespoons milk
1 teaspoon vanilla extract
Cooking spray

Preheat the air fryer to 164ºC. Spritz a cake pan with cooking spray. Combine the flour, baking powder, and salt in a large bowl. Stir to mix well. Whip the sugar and butter in a separate bowl with a hand mixer on medium speed for 3 minutes. Whip the eggs, egg yolk, milk, and vanilla extract into the sugar and butter mix with a hand mixer. Pour in the flour mixture and whip with hand mixer until sanity and smooth. Scrape the batter into the cake pan and level the batter with a spatula. Place the cake pan in the preheated air fryer. Bake for 20 minutes or until a toothpick inserted in the centre comes out clean. Check the doneness during the last 5 minutes of the baking. Invert the cake on a cooling rack and allow to cool for 15 minutes before slicing to serve.

Golden Salmon and Carrot Croquettes

Prep time: 15 minutes | Cook time: 10 minutes | Serves 6

2 egg whites
235 ml almond flour
235 ml panko breadcrumbs
450 g chopped salmon fillet
160 ml grated carrots
2 tablespoons minced garlic cloves
120 ml chopped onion
2 tablespoons chopped chives
Cooking spray

Preheat the air fryer to 176ºC. Spritz the air fryer basket with cooking spray. Whisk the egg whites in a bowl. Put the flour in a second bowl. Pour the breadcrumbs in a third bowl. Set aside. Combine the salmon, carrots, garlic, onion, and chives in a large bowl. Stir to mix well. Form the mixture into balls with your hands. Dredge the balls into the flour, then egg, and then breadcrumbs to coat well. Arrange the salmon balls in the preheated air fryer and spritz with cooking spray. Air fry for 10 minutes or until crispy and browned. Shake the basket halfway through. Serve immediately.

Eggnog Bread

Prep time: 10 minutes | Cook time: 18 minutes | Serves 6 to 8

235 ml flour, plus more for dusting
60 ml sugar
1 teaspoon baking powder
¼ teaspoon salt
¼ teaspoon nutmeg
120 ml eggnog
1 egg yolk

1 tablespoon plus 1 teaspoon butter, melted
60 ml pecans
60 ml chopped candied fruit (cherries, pineapple, or mixed fruits)
Cooking spray

Preheat the air fryer to 182ºC. In a medium bowl, stir together the flour, sugar, baking powder, salt, and nutmeg. Add eggnog, egg yolk, and butter. Mix well but do not beat. Stir in nuts and fruit. Spray a baking pan with cooking spray and dust with flour. Spread batter into prepared pan and bake for 18 minutes or until top is dark golden brown and bread starts to pull away from sides of pan. Serve immediately.

Simple Baked Green Beans

Prep time: 5 minutes | Cook time: 10 minutes | Makes 475 ml

½ teaspoon lemon pepper
2 teaspoons granulated garlic
½ teaspoon salt

1 tablespoon olive oil
475 ml fresh green beans, trimmed and snapped in half

Preheat the air fryer to 188ºC. Combine the lemon pepper, garlic, salt, and olive oil in a bowl. Stir to mix well. Add the green beans to the bowl of mixture and toss to coat well. Arrange the green beans in the preheated air fryer. Bake for 10 minutes or until tender and crispy. Shake the basket halfway through to make sure the green beans are cooked evenly. Serve immediately.

Jewish Blintzes

Prep time: 5 minutes | Cook time: 10 minutes | Makes 8 blintzes

2 (213 g) packages farmer or ricotta cheese, mashed
60 ml soft white cheese
¼ teaspoon vanilla extract

60 ml granulated white sugar
8 egg roll wrappers
4 tablespoons butter, melted

Preheat the air fryer to 192ºC. Combine the cheese, soft white cheese, vanilla extract, and sugar in a bowl. Stir to mix well. Unfold the egg roll wrappers on a clean work surface, spread 60 ml filling at the edge of each wrapper and leave a ½-inch edge uncovering. Wet the edges of the wrappers with water and fold the uncovered edge over the filling. Fold the left and right sides in the centre, then tuck the edge under the filling and fold to wrap the filling. Brush the wrappers with melted butter, then arrange the wrappers in a single layer in the preheated air fryer, seam side down. Leave a little space between each two wrappers. Work in batches to avoid overcrowding. Air fry for 10 minutes or until golden brown. Serve immediately.

Hearty Honey Yeast Rolls

Prep time: 10 minutes | Cook time: 20 minutes | Makes 8 rolls

60 ml whole milk, heated to 46ºC in the microwave
½ teaspoon active dry yeast
1 tablespoon honey
160 ml plain flour, plus more for dusting

½ teaspoon rock salt
2 tablespoons unsalted butter, at room temperature, plus more for greasing
Flaky sea salt, to taste

In a large bowl, whisk together the milk, yeast, and honey and let stand until foamy, about 10 minutes. Stir in the flour and salt until just combined. Stir in the butter until absorbed. Scrape the dough onto a lightly floured work surface and knead until smooth, about 6 minutes. Transfer the dough to a lightly greased bowl, cover loosely with a sheet of plastic wrap or a kitchen towel, and let sit until nearly doubled in size, about 1 hour. Uncover the dough, lightly press it down to expel the bubbles, then portion it into 8 equal pieces. Prep the work surface by wiping it clean with a damp paper towel (if there is flour on the work surface, it will prevent the dough from sticking lightly to the surface, which helps it form a ball). Roll each piece into a ball by cupping the palm of the hand around the dough against the work surface and moving the heel of the hand in a circular motion while using the thumb to contain the dough and tighten it into a perfectly round ball. Once all the balls are formed, nestle them side by side in the air fryer basket. Cover the rolls loosely with a kitchen towel or a sheet of plastic wrap and let sit until lightly risen and puffed, 20 to 30 minutes. Preheat the air fryer to 132ºC. Uncover the rolls and gently brush with more butter, being careful not to press the rolls too hard. Air fry until the rolls are light golden brown and fluffy, about 12 minutes. Remove the rolls from the air fryer and brush liberally with more butter, if you like, and sprinkle each roll with a pinch of sea salt. Serve warm.

Teriyaki Shrimp Skewers

Prep time: 10 minutes | Cook time: 6 minutes | Makes 12 skewered shrimp

1½ tablespoons mirin
1½ teaspoons ginger paste
1½ tablespoons soy sauce
12 large shrimp, peeled and

deveined
1 large egg
180 ml panko breadcrumbs
Cooking spray

Combine the mirin, ginger paste, and soy sauce in a large bowl. Stir to mix well. Dunk the shrimp in the bowl of mirin mixture, then wrap the bowl in plastic and refrigerate for 1 hour to marinate. Preheat the air fryer to 204ºC. Spritz the air fryer basket with cooking spray. Run twelve 4-inch skewers through each shrimp. Whisk the egg in the bowl of marinade to combine well. Pour the breadcrumbs on a plate. Dredge the shrimp skewers in the egg mixture, then shake the excess off and roll over the breadcrumbs to coat well. Arrange the shrimp skewers in the preheated air fryer and spritz with cooking spray. You need to work in batches to avoid overcrowding. Air fry for 6 minutes or until the shrimp are opaque and firm. Flip the shrimp skewers halfway through. Serve immediately.

South Carolina Shrimp and Corn Bake

Prep time: 10 minutes | Cook time: 18 minutes | Serves 2

1 ear corn, husk and silk removed, cut into 2-inch rounds
227 g red potatoes, unpeeled, cut into 1-inch pieces
2 teaspoons Old Bay or all-purpose seasoning, divided
2 teaspoons vegetable oil, divided
¼ teaspoon ground black pepper
227 g large shrimps (about 12 shrimps), deveined
170 g andouille or chorizo sausage, cut into 1-inch pieces
2 garlic cloves, minced
1 tablespoon chopped fresh parsley

Preheat the air fryer to 204°C. Put the corn rounds and potatoes in a large bowl. Sprinkle with 1 teaspoon of seasoning and drizzle with vegetable oil. Toss to coat well. Transfer the corn rounds and potatoes on a baking sheet, then put in the preheated air fryer. Bake for 12 minutes or until soft and browned. Shake the basket halfway through the cooking time. Meanwhile, cut slits into the shrimps but be careful not to cut them through. Combine the shrimps, sausage, remaining seasoning, and remaining vegetable oil in the large bowl. Toss to coat well. When the baking of the potatoes and corn rounds is complete, add the shrimps and sausage and bake for 6 more minutes or until the shrimps are opaque. Shake the basket halfway through the cooking time. When the baking is finished, serve them on a plate and spread with parsley before serving.

Frico

Prep time: 5 minutes | Cook time: 5 minutes | Serves 2

235 ml shredded aged Manchego cheese
1 teaspoon plain flour
½ teaspoon cumin seeds
¼ teaspoon cracked black pepper

Preheat the air fryer to 192°C. Line the air fryer basket with parchment paper. Combine the cheese and flour in a bowl. Stir to mix well. Spread the mixture in the basket into a 4-inch round. Combine the cumin and black pepper in a small bowl. Stir to mix well. Sprinkle the cumin mixture over the cheese round. Air fry 5 minutes or until the cheese is lightly browned and frothy. Use tongs to transfer the cheese wafer onto a plate and slice to serve.

Arancini

Prep time: 5 minutes | Cook time: 30 minutes | Makes 10 arancini

160 ml raw white Arborio rice
2 teaspoons butter
½ teaspoon salt
315 ml water
2 large eggs, well beaten
300 ml dried breadcrumbs
mixed with Italian-style seasoning
10 ¾-inch semi-firm Mozzarella cubes
Cooking spray

Pour the rice, butter, salt, and water in a pot. Stir to mix well and bring a boil over medium-high heat. Keep stirring. Reduce the heat to low and cover the pot. Simmer for 20 minutes or until the rice is tender. Turn off the heat and let sit, covered, for 10 minutes, then open the lid and fluffy the rice with a fork. Allow to cool for 10 more minutes. Preheat the air fryer to 192°C. Pour the beaten eggs in a bowl, then pour the breadcrumbs in a separate bowl. Scoop 2 tablespoons of the cooked rice up and form it into a ball, then press the Mozzarella into the ball and wrap. Dredge the ball in the eggs first, then shake the excess off the dunk the ball in the breadcrumbs. Roll to coat evenly. Repeat to make 10 balls in total with remaining rice. Transfer the balls in the preheated air fryer and spritz with cooking spray. You need to work in batches to avoid overcrowding. Air fry for 10 minutes or until the balls are lightly browned and crispy. Remove the balls from the air fryer and allow to cool before serving.

Fried Dill Pickles with Buttermilk Dressing

Prep time: 45 minutes | Cook time: 8 minutes | Serves 6 to 8

Buttermilk Dressing:
60 ml buttermilk
60 ml chopped spring onions
180 ml mayonnaise
120 ml sour cream
½ teaspoon cayenne pepper
½ teaspoon onion powder
½ teaspoon garlic powder
1 tablespoon chopped chives
2 tablespoons chopped fresh dill
Rock salt and ground black
pepper, to taste
Fried Dill Pickles:
180 ml plain flour
1 (900 g) jar kosher dill pickles, cut into 4 spears, drained
600 ml panko breadcrumbs
2 eggs, beaten with 2 tablespoons water
Rock salt and ground black pepper, to taste
Cooking spray

Preheat the air fryer to 204°C. Combine the ingredients for the dressing in a bowl. Stir to mix well. Wrap the bowl in plastic and refrigerate for 30 minutes or until ready to serve. Pour the flour in a bowl and sprinkle with salt and ground black pepper. Stir to mix well. Put the breadcrumbs in a separate bowl. Pour the beaten eggs in a third bowl. Dredge the pickle spears in the flour, then into the eggs, and then into the panko to coat well. Shake the excess off. Arrange the pickle spears in a single layer in the preheated air fryer and spritz with cooking spray. Air fry for 8 minutes. Flip the pickle spears halfway through. Serve the pickle spears with buttermilk dressing.

Spicy Air Fried Old Bay Shrimp

Prep time: 7 minutes | Cook time: 10 minutes | Makes 475 ml

½ teaspoon Old Bay or all-purpose seasoning
1 teaspoon ground cayenne pepper
½ teaspoon paprika
1 tablespoon olive oil
⅛ teaspoon salt
230 g shrimps, peeled and deveined
Juice of half a lemon

Preheat the air fryer to 200°C. Combine the seasoning, cayenne pepper, paprika, olive oil, and salt in a large bowl, then add the shrimps and toss to coat well. Put the shrimps in the preheated air fryer. Air fry for 10 minutes or until opaque. Flip the shrimps halfway through. Serve the shrimps with lemon juice on top.

Simple Air Fried Crispy Brussels Sprouts

Prep time: 5 minutes | Cook time: 20 minutes | Serves 4

¼ teaspoon salt
⅛ teaspoon ground black pepper
1 tablespoon extra-virgin olive oil

450 g Brussels sprouts, trimmed and halved
Lemon wedges, for garnish

Preheat the air fryer to 176°C. Combine the salt, black pepper, and olive oil in a large bowl. Stir to mix well. Add the Brussels sprouts to the bowl of mixture and toss to coat well. Arrange the Brussels sprouts in the preheated air fryer. Air fry for 20 minutes or until lightly browned and wilted. Shake the basket two times during the air frying. Transfer the cooked Brussels sprouts to a large plate and squeeze the lemon wedges on top to serve.

Easy Cinnamon Toast

Prep time: 5 minutes | Cook time: 20 minutes | Serves 6

1½ teaspoons cinnamon
1½ teaspoons vanilla extract
120 ml sugar
2 teaspoons ground black

pepper
2 tablespoons melted coconut oil
12 slices wholemeal bread

Preheat the air fryer to 204°C. Combine all the ingredients, except for the bread, in a large bowl. Stir to mix well. Dunk the bread in the bowl of mixture gently to coat and infuse well. Shake the excess off. Arrange the bread slices in the preheated air fryer. Air fry for 5 minutes or until golden brown. Flip the bread halfway through. You may need to cook in batches to avoid overcrowding. Remove the bread slices from the air fryer and slice to serve.

Crispy Potato Chips with Lemony Cream Dip

Prep time: 20 minutes | Cook time: 15 minutes | Serves 2 to 4

2 large russet or Maris Piper potatoes, sliced into ⅛-inch slices, rinsed
Sea salt and freshly ground black pepper, to taste
Cooking spray
Lemony Cream Dip:
120 ml sour cream

¼ teaspoon lemon juice
2 spring onions, white part only, minced
1 tablespoon olive oil
¼ teaspoon salt
Freshly ground black pepper, to taste

Soak the potato slices in water for 10 minutes, then pat dry with paper towels. Preheat the air fryer to 152°C. Transfer the potato slices in the preheated air fryer. Spritz the slices with cooking spray. You may need to work in batches to avoid overcrowding. Air fry for 15 minutes or until crispy and golden brown. Shake the basket periodically. Sprinkle with salt and ground black pepper in the last minute. Meanwhile, combine the ingredients for the dip in a small bowl. Stir to mix well. Serve the potato chips immediately with the dip.

Garlicky Baked Cherry Tomatoes

Prep time: 5 minutes | Cook time: 4 to 6 minutes | Serves 2

475 ml cherry tomatoes
1 clove garlic, thinly sliced
1 teaspoon olive oil
⅛ teaspoon rock salt

1 tablespoon freshly chopped basil, for topping
Cooking spray

Preheat the air fryer to 182°C. Spritz the air fryer baking pan with cooking spray and set aside. In a large bowl, toss together the cherry tomatoes, sliced garlic, olive oil, and rock salt. Spread the mixture in an even layer in the prepared pan. Bake in the preheated air fryer for 4 to 6 minutes, or until the tomatoes become soft and wilted. Transfer to a bowl and rest for 5 minutes. Top with the chopped basil and serve warm.

Lemony and Garlicky Asparagus

Prep time: 5 minutes | Cook time: 10 minutes | Makes 10 spears

10 spears asparagus (about 230 g in total), snap the ends off
1 tablespoon lemon juice
2 teaspoons minced garlic

½ teaspoon salt
¼ teaspoon ground black pepper
Cooking spray

Preheat the air fryer to 204°C. Line a parchment paper in the air fryer basket. Put the asparagus spears in a large bowl. Drizzle with lemon juice and sprinkle with minced garlic, salt, and ground black pepper. Toss to coat well. Transfer the asparagus in the preheated air fryer and spritz with cooking spray. Air fryer for 10 minutes or until wilted and soft. Flip the asparagus halfway through. Serve immediately.

Garlicky Zoodles

Prep time: 10 minutes | Cook time: 10 minutes | Serves 4

2 large courgette, peeled and spiralized
2 large yellow butternut squash, peeled and spiralized
1 tablespoon olive oil, divided

½ teaspoon rock salt
1 garlic clove, whole
2 tablespoons fresh basil, chopped
Cooking spray

Preheat the air fryer to 182°C. Spritz the air fryer basket with cooking spray. Combine the courgette and butternut squash with 1 teaspoon olive oil and salt in a large bowl. Toss to coat well. Transfer the courgette and butternut squash in the preheated air fryer and add the garlic. Air fry for 10 minutes or until tender and fragrant. Toss the spiralized courgette and butternut squash halfway through the cooking time. Transfer the cooked courgette and butternut squash onto a plate and set aside. Remove the garlic from the air fryer and allow to cool for a few minutes. Mince the garlic and combine with remaining olive oil in a small bowl. Stir to mix well. Drizzle the spiralized courgette and butternut squash with garlic oil and sprinkle with basil. Toss to serve.

Chapter 10 Desserts

Chapter 10 Desserts

Strawberry Shortcake

Prep time: 10 minutes | Cook time: 25 minutes | Serves 6

2 tablespoons coconut oil
110 g blanched finely ground almond flour
2 large eggs, whisked
100 g granulated sweetener
1 teaspoon baking powder
1 teaspoon vanilla extract
240 g heavy cream, whipped
6 medium fresh strawberries, hulled and sliced

In a large bowl, combine coconut oil, flour, eggs, sweetener, baking powder, and vanilla. Pour batter into an ungreased round nonstick baking dish. Place dish into air fryer basket. Adjust the temperature to 148°C and bake for 25 minutes. When done, shortcake should be golden, and a toothpick inserted in the middle will come out clean. Remove dish from fryer and let cool 1 hour. Once cooled, top cake with whipped cream and strawberries to serve.

Cinnamon Cupcakes with Cream Cheese Frosting

Prep time: 10 minutes | Cook time: 20 to 25 minutes | Serves 6

50 g almond flour, plus 2 tablespoons
2 tablespoons low-carb vanilla protein powder
⅛ teaspoon salt
1 teaspoon baking powder
¼ teaspoon ground cinnamon
55 g unsalted butter
25 g powdered sweetener
2 eggs
½ teaspoon vanilla extract
2 tablespoons heavy cream
Cream Cheese Frosting:
110 g cream cheese, softened
2 tablespoons unsalted butter, softened
½ teaspoon vanilla extract
2 tablespoons powdered sweetener
1 to 2 tablespoons heavy cream

Preheat the air fryer to 160°C. Lightly coat 6 silicone muffin cups with oil and set aside. In a medium bowl, combine the almond flour, protein powder, salt, baking powder, and cinnamon; set aside. In a stand mixer fitted with a paddle attachment, beat the butter and sweetener until creamy. Add the eggs, vanilla, and heavy cream, and beat again until thoroughly combined. Add half the flour mixture at a time to the butter mixture, mixing after each addition, until you have a smooth, creamy batter. Divide the batter evenly among the muffin cups, filling each one about three-fourths full. Arrange the muffin cups in the air fryer and air fry for 20 to 25 minutes, or until a toothpick inserted into the center of a cupcake comes out clean. Transfer the cupcakes to a rack and let cool completely. To make the cream cheese frosting: In a stand mixer fitted with a paddle attachment, beat the cream cheese, butter, and vanilla until fluffy. Add the sweetener and mix again until thoroughly combined. With the mixer running, add the heavy cream a tablespoon at a time until the frosting is smooth and creamy. Frost the cupcakes as desired.

Pecan Brownies

Prep time: 10 minutes | Cook time: 20 minutes | Serves 6

50 g blanched finely ground almond flour
55 g powdered sweetener
2 tablespoons unsweetened cocoa powder
½ teaspoon baking powder
55 g unsalted butter, softened
1 large egg
35 g chopped pecans
40 g low-carb, sugar-free chocolate chips

In a large bowl, mix almond flour, sweetener, cocoa powder, and baking powder. Stir in butter and egg. Fold in pecans and chocolate chips. Scoop mixture into a round baking pan. Place pan into the air fryer basket. Adjust the temperature to 148°C and bake for 20 minutes. When fully cooked a toothpick inserted in center will come out clean. Allow 20 minutes to fully cool and firm up.

Strawberry Pastry Rolls

Prep time: 20 minutes | Cook time: 5 to 6 minutes per batch | Serves 4

85 g low-fat cream cheese
2 tablespoons plain yogurt
2 teaspoons granulated sugar
¼ teaspoon pure vanilla extract
225 g fresh strawberries
8 sheets filo pastry
Butter-flavored cooking spray
45-90 g dark chocolate chips (optional)

In a medium bowl, combine the cream cheese, yogurt, sugar, and vanilla. Beat with hand mixer at high speed until smooth (about 1 minute). Wash strawberries and destem. Chop enough of them to measure 80 g. Stir into cheese mixture. Preheat the air fryer to 164°C. Filo pastry dries out quickly, so cover your stack of filo sheets with baking paper and then place a damp dish towel on top of that. Remove only one sheet at a time as you work. To create one pastry roll, lay out a single sheet of filo. Spray lightly with butter-flavored spray, top with a second sheet of filo and spray the second sheet lightly. Place a quarter of the filling (about 3 tablespoons) about ½ inch from the edge of one short side. Fold the end of the pastry over the filling and keep rolling a turn or two. Fold in both the left and right sides so that the edges meet in the middle of your roll. Then roll up completely. Spray outside of pastry roll with butter spray. When you have 4 rolls, place them in the air fryer basket, seam side down, leaving some space in between each. Air fry for 5 to 6 minutes, until they turn a delicate golden brown. Repeat step 7 for remaining rolls. Allow pastries to cool to room temperature. 1When ready to serve, slice the remaining strawberries. If desired, melt the chocolate chips in microwave or double boiler. Place 1 pastry on each dessert plate, and top with sliced strawberries. Drizzle melted chocolate over strawberries and onto plate.

Baked Brazilian Pineapple

Prep time: 10 minutes | Cook time: 10 minutes | Serves 4

95 g brown sugar
2 teaspoons ground cinnamon
1 small pineapple, peeled,

cored, and cut into spears
3 tablespoons unsalted butter, melted

In a small bowl, mix the brown sugar and cinnamon until thoroughly combined. Brush the pineapple spears with the melted butter. Sprinkle the cinnamon-sugar over the spears, pressing lightly to ensure it adheres well. Place the spears in the air fryer basket in a single layer. (Depending on the size of your air fryer, you may have to do this in batches.) Set the air fryer to 204°C and cook for 10 minutes for the first batch (6 to 8 minutes for the next batch, as the fryer will be preheated). Halfway through the cooking time, brush the spears with butter. The pineapple spears are done when they are heated through, and the sugar is bubbling. Serve hot.

Gluten-Free Spice Cookies

Prep time: 10 minutes | Cook time: 12 minutes | Serves 4

4 tablespoons unsalted butter, at room temperature
2 tablespoons agave nectar
1 large egg
2 tablespoons water
240 g almond flour
100 g granulated sugar

2 teaspoons ground ginger
1 teaspoon ground cinnamon
½ teaspoon freshly grated nutmeg
1 teaspoon baking soda
¼ teaspoon kosher, or coarse sea salt

Line the bottom of the air fryer basket with baking paper cut to fit. In a large bowl, using a hand mixer, beat together the butter, agave, egg, and water on medium speed until light and fluffy. Add the almond flour, sugar, ginger, cinnamon, nutmeg, baking soda, and salt. Beat on low speed until well combined. Roll the dough into 2-tablespoon balls and arrange them on the baking paper in the basket. (They don't really spread too much but try to leave a little room between them.) Set the air fryer to 164°C, and cook for 12 minutes, or until the tops of cookies are lightly browned. Transfer to a wire rack and let cool completely. Store in an airtight container for up to a week.

Pecan Bars

Prep time: 5 minutes | Cook time: 40 minutes | Serves 12

220 g coconut flour
5 tablespoons granulated sweetener
4 tablespoons coconut oil,

softened
60 ml heavy cream
1 egg, beaten
4 pecans, chopped

Mix coconut flour, sweetener, coconut oil, heavy cream, and egg. Pour the batter in the air fryer basket and flatten well. Top the mixture with pecans and cook the meal at 176°C for 40 minutes. Cut the cooked meal into the bars.

Pecan Butter Cookies

Prep time: 5 minutes | Cook time: 24 minutes | Makes 12 cookies

125 g chopped pecans
110 g salted butter, melted
55 g coconut flour

150 g granulated sweetener, divided
1 teaspoon vanilla extract

In a food processor, blend together pecans, butter, flour, 100 g sweetener, and vanilla 1 minute until a dough forms. Form dough into twelve individual cookie balls, about 1 tablespoon each. Cut three pieces of baking paper to fit air fryer basket. Place four cookies on each ungreased baking paper and place one piece baking paper with cookies into air fryer basket. Adjust air fryer temperature to 164°C and set the timer for 8 minutes. Repeat cooking with remaining batches. When the timer goes off, allow cookies to cool 5 minutes on a large serving plate until cool enough to handle. While still warm, dust cookies with remaining granulated sweetener. Allow to cool completely, about 15 minutes, before serving.

Old-Fashioned Fudge Pie

Prep time: 15 minutes | Cook time: 25 to 30 minutes | Serves 8

300 g granulated sugar
40 g unsweetened cocoa powder
70 g self-raising flour
3 large eggs, unbeaten
12 tablespoons unsalted butter,

melted
1½ teaspoons vanilla extract
1 (9-inch) unbaked piecrust
30 g icing sugar (optional)

In a medium bowl, stir together the sugar, cocoa powder, and flour. Stir in the eggs and melted butter. Stir in the vanilla. Preheat the air fryer to 176°C. Pour the chocolate filing into the crust. Cook for 25 to 30 minutes, stirring every 10 minutes, until a knife inserted into the middle comes out clean. Let sit for 5 minutes before dusting with icing sugar (if using) to serve.

Caramelized Fruit Skewers

Prep time: 10 minutes | Cook time: 3 to 5 minutes | Serves 4

2 peaches, peeled, pitted, and thickly sliced
3 plums, halved and pitted
3 nectarines, halved and pitted
1 tablespoon honey

½ teaspoon ground cinnamon
¼ teaspoon ground allspice
Pinch cayenne pepper
Special Equipment:
8 metal skewers

Preheat the air fryer to 204°C. Thread, alternating peaches, plums, and nectarines, onto the metal skewers that fit into the air fryer. Thoroughly combine the honey, cinnamon, allspice, and cayenne in a small bowl. Brush the glaze generously over the fruit skewers. Transfer the fruit skewers to the air fryer basket. You may need to cook in batches to avoid overcrowding. Air fry for 3 to 5 minutes, or until the fruit is caramelized. Remove from the basket and repeat with the remaining fruit skewers. Let the fruit skewers rest for 5 minutes before serving.

Cream Cheese Danish

Prep time: 20 minutes | Cook time: 15 minutes | Serves 6

70 g blanched finely ground almond flour
225 g shredded Mozzarella cheese
140 g full-fat cream cheese, divided

2 large egg yolks
75 g powdered sweetener, divided
2 teaspoons vanilla extract, divided

In a large microwave-safe bowl, add almond flour, Mozzarella, and 30 g cream cheese. Mix and then microwave for 1 minute. Stir and add egg yolks to the bowl. Continue stirring until soft dough forms. Add 50 g sweetener to dough and 1 teaspoon vanilla. Cut a piece of baking paper to fit your air fryer basket. Wet your hands with warm water and press out the dough into a ¼-inch-thick rectangle. In a medium bowl, mix remaining cream cheese, remaining sweetener, and vanilla. Place this cream cheese mixture on the right half of the dough rectangle. Fold over the left side of the dough and press to seal. Place into the air fryer basket. Adjust the temperature to 164°C and bake for 15 minutes. After 7 minutes, flip over the Danish. When done, remove the Danish from baking paper and allow to completely cool before cutting.

Shortcut Spiced Apple Butter

Prep time: 5 minutes | Cook time: 1 hour | Makes 1¼ cups

Cooking spray
500 g store-bought unsweetened applesauce
130 g packed light brown sugar
3 tablespoons fresh lemon juice

½ teaspoon kosher, or coarse sea salt
¼ teaspoon ground cinnamon
⅛ teaspoon ground allspice

Spray a cake pan with cooking spray. Whisk together all the ingredients in a bowl until smooth, then pour into the greased pan. Set the pan in the air fryer and bake at 172°C until the apple mixture is caramelized, reduced to a thick purée, and fragrant, about 1 hour. Remove the pan from the air fryer, stir to combine the caramelized bits at the edge with the rest, then let cool completely to thicken. Scrape the apple butter into a jar and store in the refrigerator for up to 2 weeks.

Lemon Curd Pavlova

Prep time: 10 minutes | Cook time: 1 hour | Serves 4

Shell:
3 large egg whites
¼ teaspoon cream of tartar
75 g powdered sweetener
1 teaspoon grated lemon zest
1 teaspoon lemon extract
Lemon Curd:

100 g powdered sweetener
120 ml lemon juice
4 large eggs
120 ml coconut oil
For Garnish (Optional):
Blueberries
powdered sweetener

Preheat the air fryer to 135°C. Thoroughly grease a pie pan with butter or coconut oil. Make the shell: In a small bowl, use a hand mixer to beat the egg whites and cream of tartar until soft peaks form. With the mixer on low, slowly sprinkle in the sweetener and mix until it's completely incorporated. Add the lemon zest and lemon extract and continue to beat with the hand mixer until stiff peaks form. Spoon the mixture into the greased pie pan, then smooth it across the bottom, up the sides, and onto the rim to form a shell. Bake for 1 hour, then turn off the air fryer and let the shell stand in the air fryer for 20 minutes. (The shell can be made up to 3 days ahead and stored in an airtight container in the refrigerator, if desired.) While the shell bakes, make the lemon curd: In a medium-sized heavy-bottomed saucepan, whisk together the sweetener, lemon juice, and eggs. Add the coconut oil and place the pan on the stovetop over medium heat. Once the oil is melted, whisk constantly until the mixture thickens and thickly coats the back of a spoon, about 10 minutes. Do not allow the mixture to come to a boil. Pour the lemon curd mixture through a fine-mesh strainer into a medium-sized bowl. Place the bowl inside a larger bowl filled with ice water and whisk occasionally until the curd is completely cool, about 15 minutes. Place the lemon curd on top of the shell and garnish with blueberries and powdered sweetener, if desired. Store leftovers in the refrigerator for up to 4 days.

Almond Shortbread

Prep time: 10 minutes | Cook time: 12 minutes | Serves 8

110 g unsalted butter
100 g granulated sugar

1 teaspoon pure almond extract
125 g plain flour

In bowl of a stand mixer fitted with the paddle attachment, beat the butter and sugar on medium speed until light and fluffy (3 to 4 minutes). Add the almond extract and beat until combined (about 30 seconds). Turn the mixer to low. Add the flour a little at a time and beat for about 2 minutes more until well-incorporated. Pat the dough into an even layer in a baking pan. Place the pan in the air fryer basket. Set the air fryer to 192°C and bake for 12 minutes. Carefully remove the pan from air fryer basket. While the shortbread is still warm and soft, cut it into 8 wedges. Let cool in the pan on a wire rack for 5 minutes. Remove the wedges from the pan and let cool completely on the rack before serving.

Pecan and Cherry Stuffed Apples

Prep time: 10 minutes | Cook time: 20 minutes | Serves 4

4 apples (about 565 g)
40 g chopped pecans
50 g dried tart cherries
1 tablespoon melted butter

3 tablespoons brown sugar
¼ teaspoon allspice
Pinch salt
Ice cream, for serving

Cut off top ½ inch from each apple; reserve tops. With a melon baller, core through stem ends without breaking through the bottom. (Do not trim bases.) Preheat the air fryer to 176°C. Combine pecans, cherries, butter, brown sugar, allspice, and a pinch of salt. Stuff mixture into the hollow centers of the apples. Cover with apple tops. Put in the air fryer basket, using tongs. Air fry for 20 to 25 minutes, or just until tender. Serve warm with ice cream.

Butter Flax Cookies

Prep time: 25 minutes | Cook time: 20 minutes | Serves 4

225 g almond meal
2 tablespoons flaxseed meal
30 g monk fruit, or equivalent sweetener
1 teaspoon baking powder
A pinch of grated nutmeg

A pinch of coarse salt
1 large egg, room temperature.
110 g unsalted butter, room temperature
1 teaspoon vanilla extract

Mix the almond meal, flaxseed meal, monk fruit, baking powder, grated nutmeg, and salt in a bowl. In a separate bowl, whisk the egg, butter, and vanilla extract. Stir the egg mixture into dry mixture; mix to combine well or until it forms a nice, soft dough. Roll your dough out and cut out with a cookie cutter of your choice. Bake in the preheated air fryer at 176°C for 10 minutes. Decrease the temperature to 164°C and cook for 10 minutes longer. Bon appétit!

Almond-Roasted Pears

Prep time: 10 minutes | Cook time: 15 to 20 minutes | Serves 4

Yogurt Topping:
140-170 g pot vanilla Greek yogurt
¼ teaspoon almond flavoring

2 whole pears
4 crushed Biscoff biscuits
1 tablespoon flaked almonds
1 tablespoon unsalted butter

Stir the almond flavoring into yogurt and set aside while preparing pears. Halve each pear and spoon out the core. Place pear halves in air fryer basket, skin side down. Stir together the crushed biscuits and almonds. Place a quarter of this mixture into the hollow of each pear half. Cut butter into 4 pieces and place one piece on top of biscuit mixture in each pear. Roast at 184°C for 15 to 20 minutes, or until pears have cooked through but are still slightly firm. Serve pears warm with a dollop of yogurt topping.

Biscuit-Base Cheesecake

Prep time: 10 minutes | Cook time: 20 minutes | Serves 8

100 g crushed digestive biscuits
3 tablespoons butter, at room temperature
225 g cream cheese, at room temperature

65 g granulated sugar
2 eggs, beaten
1 tablespoon all-purpose flour
1 teaspoon vanilla extract
60 ml chocolate syrup

In a small bowl, stir together the crushed biscuits and butter. Press the crust into the bottom of a 6-by-2-inch round baking pan and freeze to set while you prepare the filling. In a medium bowl, stir together the cream cheese and sugar until mixed well. One at a time, beat in the eggs. Add the flour and vanilla and stir to combine. Transfer ⅓ of the filling to a small bowl and stir in the chocolate syrup until combined. Insert the crisper plate into the basket and the basket into the unit. Preheat the air fryer to 164°C, and bake for 3 minutes. Pour the vanilla filling into the pan with the crust. Drop the chocolate filling over the vanilla filling by the spoonful. With a clean butter knife stir the fillings in a zigzag pattern to marble them. Do not let the knife touch the crust. Once the unit is preheated, place the pan into the basket. Set the temperature to 164°C, and bake for 20 minutes. When the cooking is done, the cheesecake should be just set. Cool on a wire rack for 1 hour. Refrigerate the cheesecake until firm before slicing.

Apple Wedges with Apricots

Prep time: 5 minutes | Cook time: 15 to 18 minutes | Serves 4

4 large apples, peeled and sliced into 8 wedges
2 tablespoons light olive oil
95 g dried apricots, chopped

1 to 2 tablespoons granulated sugar
½ teaspoon ground cinnamon

Preheat the air fryer to 180°C. Toss the apple wedges with the olive oil in a mixing bowl until well coated. Place the apple wedges in the air fryer basket and air fry for 12 to 15 minutes. Sprinkle with the dried apricots and air fry for another 3 minutes. Meanwhile, thoroughly combine the sugar and cinnamon in a small bowl. Remove the apple wedges from the basket to a plate. Serve sprinkled with the sugar mixture.

Molten Chocolate Almond Cakes

Prep time: 5 minutes | Cook time: 13 minutes | Serves 3

Butter and flour for the ramekins
110 g bittersweet chocolate, chopped
110 gunsalted butter
2 eggs
2 egg yolks
50 g granulated sugar
½ teaspoon pure vanilla extract, or almond extract

1 tablespoon plain flour
3 tablespoons ground almonds
8 to 12 semisweet chocolate discs (or 4 chunks of chocolate)
Cocoa powder or icing sugar, for dusting
Toasted almonds, coarsely chopped

Butter and flour three (170 g) ramekins. (Butter the ramekins and then coat the butter with flour by shaking it around in the ramekin and dumping out any excess.) Melt the chocolate and butter together, either in the microwave or in a double boiler. In a separate bowl, beat the eggs, egg yolks and sugar together until light and smooth. Add the vanilla extract. Whisk the chocolate mixture into the egg mixture. Stir in the flour and ground almonds. Preheat the air fryer to 164°C. Transfer the batter carefully to the buttered ramekins, filling halfway. Place two or three chocolate discs in the center of the batter and then fill the ramekins to ½-inch below the top with the remaining batter. Place the ramekins into the air fryer basket and air fry for 13 minutes. The sides of the cake should be set, but the centers should be slightly soft. Remove the ramekins from the air fryer and let the cakes sit for 5 minutes. (If you'd like the cake a little less molten, air fry for 14 minutes and let the cakes sit for 4 minutes.) Run a butter knife around the edge of the ramekins and invert the cakes onto a plate. Lift the ramekin off the plate slowly and carefully so that the cake doesn't break. Dust with cocoa powder or icing sugar and serve with a scoop of ice cream and some coarsely chopped toasted almonds.

Chickpea Brownies

Prep time: 10 minutes | Cook time: 20 minutes | Serves 6

Vegetable oil
425 g can chickpeas, drained and rinsed
4 large eggs
80 ml coconut oil, melted
80 ml honey
3 tablespoons unsweetened

cocoa powder
1 tablespoon espresso powder (optional)
1 teaspoon baking powder
1 teaspoon baking soda
80 g chocolate chips

Preheat the air fryer to 164ºC. Generously grease a baking pan with vegetable oil. In a blender or food processor, combine the chickpeas, eggs, coconut oil, honey, cocoa powder, espresso powder (if using), baking powder, and baking soda. Blend or process until smooth. Transfer to the prepared pan and stir in the chocolate chips by hand. Set the pan in the air fryer basket and bake for 20 minutes, or until a toothpick inserted into the center comes out clean. Let cool in the pan on a wire rack for 30 minutes before cutting into squares. Serve immediately.

Berry Crumble

Prep time: 10 minutes | Cook time: 15 minutes | Serves 4

For the Filling:
300 g mixed berries
2 tablespoons sugar
1 tablespoon cornflour
1 tablespoon fresh lemon juice
For the Topping:
30 g plain flour

20 g rolled oats
1 tablespoon granulated sugar
2 tablespoons cold unsalted butter, cut into small cubes
Whipped cream or ice cream (optional)

Preheat the air fryer to 204ºC. For the filling: In a round baking pan, gently mix the berries, sugar, cornflour, and lemon juice until thoroughly combined. For the topping: In a small bowl, combine the flour, oats, and sugar. Stir the butter into the flour mixture until the mixture has the consistency of breadcrumbs. Sprinkle the topping over the berries. Put the pan in the air fryer basket and air fry for 15 minutes. Let cool for 5 minutes on a wire rack. Serve topped with whipped cream or ice cream, if desired.

Applesauce and Chocolate Brownies

Prep time: 10 minutes | Cook time: 15 minutes | Serves 8

25 g unsweetened cocoa powder
30 g plain flour
¼ teaspoon kosher, or coarse sea salt
½ teaspoons baking powder
3 tablespoons unsalted butter, melted

100 g granulated sugar
1 large egg
3 tablespoons unsweetened applesauce
50 g miniature semisweet chocolate chips
Coarse sea salt, to taste

Preheat the air fryer to 148ºC. In a large bowl, whisk together the cocoa powder, plain flour, kosher salt, and baking powder. In a separate large bowl, combine the butter, granulated sugar, egg, and applesauce, then use a spatula to fold in the cocoa powder mixture and the chocolate chips until well combined. Spray a baking pan with nonstick cooking spray, then pour the mixture into the pan. Place the pan in the air fryer and bake for 15 minutes or until a toothpick comes out clean when inserted in the middle. Remove the brownies from the air fryer, sprinkle some coarse sea salt on top, and allow to cool in the pan on a wire rack for 20 minutes before cutting and serving.

Apple Hand Pies

Prep time: 15 minutes | Cook time: 25 minutes | Serves 8

2 apples, cored and diced
60 ml honey
1 teaspoon ground cinnamon
1 teaspoon vanilla extract
⅛ teaspoon ground nutmeg

2 teaspoons cornflour
1 teaspoon water
1 sheet shortcrust pastry cut into
4
Cooking oil spray

Insert the crisper plate into the basket and the basket into the unit. Preheat the unit to 204ºC. In a metal bowl that fits into the basket, stir together the apples, honey, cinnamon, vanilla, and nutmeg. In a small bowl, whisk the cornflour and water until the cornflour dissolves. Once the unit is preheated, place the metal bowl with the apples into the basket. cook for 2 minutes then stir the apples. Resume cooking for 2 minutes. Remove the bowl and stir the cornflour mixture into the apples. Reinsert the metal bowl into the basket and resume cooking for about 30 seconds until the sauce thickens slightly. When the cooking is complete, refrigerate the apples while you prepare the piecrust. Cut each piecrust into 2 (4-inch) circles. You should have 8 circles of crust. Lay the piecrusts on a work surface. Divide the apple filling among the piecrusts, mounding the mixture in the center of each round. 1Fold each piecrust over so the top layer of crust is about an inch short of the bottom layer. (The edges should not meet.) Use the back of a fork to seal the edges. 1Insert the crisper plate into the basket and the basket into the unit. Preheat the unit 204ºC again. 1Once the unit is preheated, spray the crisper plate with cooking oil, line the basket with baking paper, and spray it with cooking oil. Working in batches, place the hand pies into the basket in a single layer. 1Cook the pies for 10 minutes. 1When the cooking is complete, let the hand pies cool for 5 minutes before removing from the basket. 1Repeat steps 12, 13, and 14 with the remaining pies.

Homemade Mint Pie

Prep time: 15 minutes | Cook time: 25 minutes | Serves 2

1 tablespoon instant coffee
2 tablespoons almond butter, softened
2 tablespoons granulated sweetener

1 teaspoon dried mint
3 eggs, beaten
1 teaspoon dried spearmint
4 teaspoons coconut flour
Cooking spray

Spray the air fryer basket with cooking spray. Then mix all ingredients in the mixer bowl. When you get a smooth mixture, transfer it in the air fryer basket. Flatten it gently. Cook the pie at 185ºC for 25 minutes.

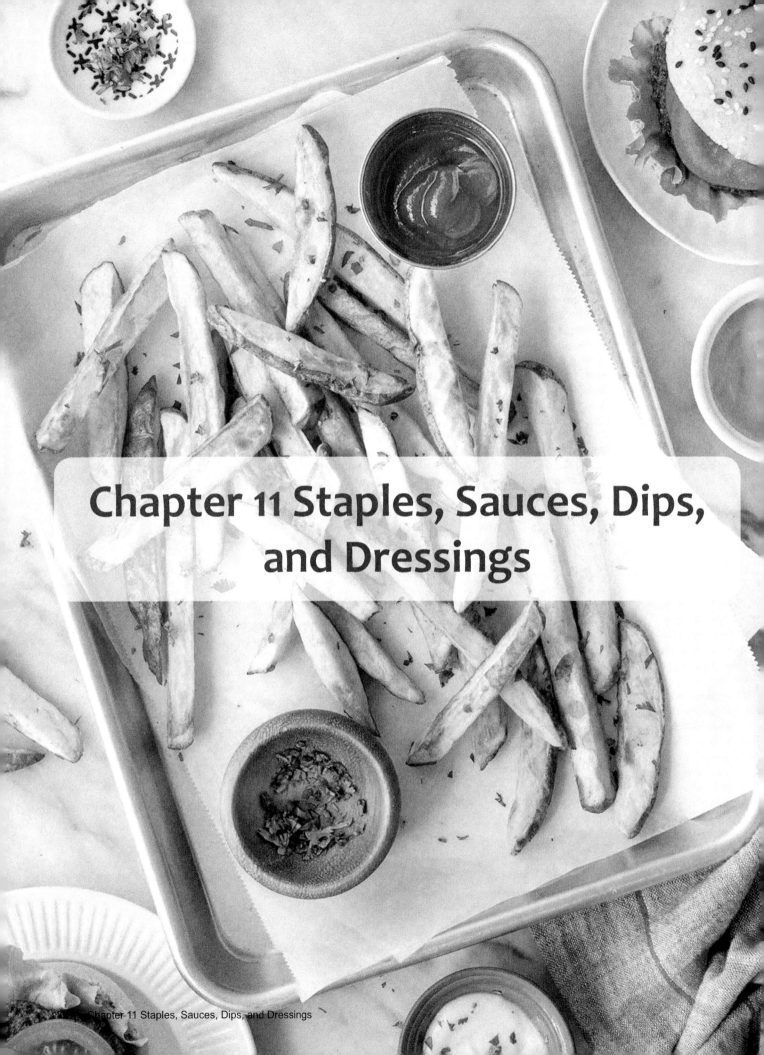

Chapter 11 Staples, Sauces, Dips, and Dressings

Chapter 11 Staples, Sauces, Dips, and Dressings

Traditional Caesar Dressing

Prep time: 10 minutes | Cook time: 5 minutes | Makes 350 ml

2 teaspoons minced garlic
4 large egg yolks
60 ml wine vinegar
½ teaspoon mustard powder
Dash Worcestershire sauce

235 ml extra-virgin olive oil
60 ml freshly squeezed lemon juice
Sea salt and freshly ground black pepper, to taste

To a small saucepan, add the garlic, egg yolks, vinegar, mustard, and Worcestershire sauce and place over low heat. Whisking constantly, cook the mixture until it thickens and is a little bubbly, about 5 minutes. Remove saucepan from the heat and let it stand for about 10 minutes to cool. Transfer the egg mixture to a large stainless-steel bowl. Whisking constantly, add the olive oil in a thin stream. Whisk in the lemon juice and season the dressing with salt and pepper. Transfer the dressing to an airtight container and keep in the refrigerator for up to 3 days.

Cucumber Yoghurt Dip

Prep time: 5 minutes | Cook time: 0 minutes | Serves 2 to 3

235 ml plain, unsweetened, full-fat Greek yoghurt
120 ml cucumber, peeled, seeded, and diced
1 tablespoon freshly squeezed

lemon juice
1 tablespoon chopped fresh mint
1 small garlic clove, minced
Salt and freshly ground black pepper, to taste

In a food processor, combine the yoghurt, cucumber, lemon juice, mint, and garlic. Pulse several times to combine, leaving noticeable cucumber chunks. Taste and season with salt and pepper.

Hot Honey Mustard Dip

Prep time: 5 minutes | Cook time: 0 minutes | Makes 315 ml

180 ml mayonnaise
80 ml spicy brown mustard

60 ml honey
½ teaspoon cayenne pepper

In a medium bowl, stir together the mayonnaise, mustard, and honey until blended. Stir in the cayenne. Cover and chill for 3 hours so the flavours blend. Keep refrigerated in an airtight container for up to 3 weeks.

Tzatziki

Prep time: 10 minutes | Cook time: 0 minutes | Serves 4

1 large cucumber, peeled and grated (about 475 ml)
235 ml plain Greek yoghurt
2 to 3 garlic cloves, minced
1 tablespoon tahini (sesame

paste)
1 tablespoon fresh lemon juice
½ teaspoon rock salt, or to taste
Chopped fresh parsley or dill, for garnish (optional)

In a medium bowl, combine the cucumber, yoghurt, garlic, tahini, lemon juice, and salt. Stir until well combined. Cover and chill until ready to serve. Right before serving, sprinkle with chopped fresh parsley, if desired.

Dijon and Balsamic Vinaigrette

Prep time: 5 minutes | Cook time: 0 minutes | Makes 12 tablespoons

6 tablespoons water
4 tablespoons Dijon mustard
4 tablespoons balsamic vinegar
1 teaspoon maple syrup

½ teaspoon pink Himalayan salt
¼ teaspoon freshly ground black pepper

In a bowl, whisk together all the ingredients.

Tomatillo Salsa for Air Fryer

Prep time: 5 minutes | Cook time: 15 minutes | Serves 4

12 tomatillos or alternatively underripe tomatoes with a dash of lime juice
2 fresh serrano chillies or jalapeños

1 tablespoon minced garlic
235 ml chopped fresh coriander leaves
1 tablespoon vegetable oil
1 teaspoon rock salt

Remove and discard the papery husks from the tomatillos and rinse them under warm running water to remove the sticky coating. Place the tomatillos and peppers in a baking pan. Place the pan in the air fryer basket. Air fry at 176°C for 15 minutes. Transfer the tomatillos and peppers to a blender, add the garlic, coriander, vegetable oil, and salt, and blend until almost smooth. (If not using immediately, omit the salt and add it just before serving.) Serve or store in an airtight container in the refrigerator for up to 10 days.

Lemon Cashew Dip

180 ml cashews, soaked in water for at least 4 hours and drained
Juice and zest of 1 lemon
60 ml water
2 tablespoons chopped fresh dill
¼ teaspoon salt, plus additional as needed

Blend the cashew, lemon juice and zest, and water in a blender until smooth and creamy. Fold in the dill and salt and blend again. Taste and add additional salt as needed. Transfer to the refrigerator to chill for at least 1 hour to blend the flavours. This dip perfectly goes with the crackers or tacos. It also can be used as a sauce for roasted vegetables, or a sandwich spread.

Air Fryer Artichoke Dip

1 (400 g) can artichoke hearts, drained
450 g goat cheese
2 tablespoons extra-virgin olive oil
2 teaspoons lemon juice
1 garlic clove, minced
1 tablespoon chopped parsley
1 tablespoon chopped chives
½ tablespoon chopped basil
½ teaspoon sea salt
½ teaspoon freshly ground black pepper
Dash of cayenne pepper (optional)
120 ml freshly grated Pecorino Romano

In a food processor, combine all the ingredients, except the Pecorino Romano, and process until well incorporated and creamy. Top with the freshly grated Pecorino Romano. Store in an airtight container in the refrigerator for up to 3 days.

Cauliflower Alfredo Sauce

2 tablespoons olive oil
6 garlic cloves, minced
700 ml unsweetened almond milk
1 (450 g) head cauliflower, cut into florets
1 teaspoon salt
¼ teaspoon freshly ground black pepper
Juice of 1 lemon
4 tablespoons Engevita yeast flakes

In a medium saucepan, heat the olive oil over medium-high heat. Add the garlic and sauté for 1 minute or until fragrant. Add the almond milk, stir, and bring to a boil. Gently add the cauliflower. Stir in the salt and pepper and return to a boil. Continue cooking over medium-high heat for 5 minutes or until the cauliflower is soft. Stir frequently and reduce heat if needed to prevent the liquid from boiling over. Carefully transfer the cauliflower and cooking liquid to a food processor, using a slotted spoon to scoop out the larger pieces of cauliflower before pouring in the liquid. Add the lemon and yeast flakes and blend for 1 to 2 minutes until smooth. Serve immediately.

Apple Cider Dressing

2 tablespoons apple cider vinegar
⅓ lemon, juiced
⅓ lemon, zested
Salt and freshly ground black pepper, to taste

In a jar, combine the vinegar, lemon juice, and zest. Season with salt and pepper, cover, and shake well.

Printed in Great Britain
by Amazon